HAUNTED HOUSES

HANS HOLZER'S
Travel Guide To
HAUNTED HOUSES

By Hans Holzer

Illustrations by
Nathan C. S. Frerichs

BLACK DOG
& LEVENTHAL
PUBLISHERS
NEW YORK

Maps by David Allen
Supplementary Research: Catharine Wood

Published by
Black Dog & Leventhal Publishers
151 W. 19th St.
New York, NY 10011

Distributed by
Workman Publishing Company
708 Broadway
New York, NY 10003

ISBN 1-57912-016-4
h g f e d c b a

Design by Jonette Jakobson

About the Author

Professor Hans Holzer, Ph.D., is the author
of 119 books on ghosts, haunted places and
parapsychology. His works include
*Life Beyond, The Directory of Psychics,
America's Mysterious Places ,Window to the Past,*
and *Ghosts: True Encounters with the World Beyond*.
He is a prominent lecturer in parapsychology
and has written, produced and hosted
several television programs.
He lives in New York City.

About the Illustrator

Nathan C.S. Frerichs exhibited a passion and talent
for art at an early age. He is currently working on
murals in Telluride, Colorado and Portland, Oregon
in addition to projects in illustration, environmental
sculpture and graphic design. His inspiration comes
from his beautiful mother, Ellen Lanier, who taught
him how to see the world.

Acknowledgments

I would like to thank my publisher,
J.P. Leventhal
and my editor, Jessica MacMurray,
for their help in making
this project possible.

TABLE OF CONTENTS

INTRODUCTION

What exactly is a ghost? In terms of psychic research, a ghost appears to be a surviving emotional memory of someone who died traumatically or tragically, but is unaware of his or her death. Those ghosts who do know are confused about where they are, or why they don't feel quite the way they used to feel. When a person has lived in a place for a very long time, acquiring certain routines and becoming very attached to the premises, sudden death comes as a shock. Unwilling to part with the physical world, those human personalities stay on at the spot where their tragedy or their emotional attachment existed prior to their physical death.

In terms of physics, ghosts are electromagnetic fields originally encased in an outer layer called the physical body. After death that outer layer dissolves, leaving the inner self free. With the majority of people, this inner self—also referred to as the soul or the psyche—will drift out into the nonphysical world where it is able to move forward or backward in time and space, motivated by thought and possessed of all earth memories fully intact. Such a free spirit is indeed a development upward, and as rational a being as he or she was on earth.

Since the dawn of mankind, people have believed in ghosts. The fear of the unknown, the certainty that there was something somewhere out there bigger than life and more powerful than anything walking the earth, has persisted throughout the ages. This concept had its origins in primitive man's thinking. To him, there were good and evil forces at work in nature, ruled by supernatural beings, and to some degree capable of being influenced by the attitudes and prayers of man. Fear of death was (and is still) one of the strongest human emotions. Although some belief in survival after physical death has existed from the beginning of recorded human history, hardly anyone ever cherished the notion of leaving this earth. Death was a menace.

An even greater threat was the return of those known to be dead. In the French language, ghosts are referred to as *les revenants*—the returning ones. To most people, ghosts are those coming back from the realms of the dead to haunt the living for some reason. My psychic research has refuted the notion that

11

ghosts are returnees from the land of the dead.

Ghosts have never harmed anyone except through fear found within the witness, through actions of his own because of ignorance as to what ghosts represent. In the few cases where ghosts have attacked people, it was simply a matter of mistaken identity, where extreme violence at the time of death has left a strong residue of memory in the individual ghost. By and large, it is entirely safe to be a ghost hunter, or to become a witness to phenomena of this kind.

Ghosts, then, are very real, and the range of people who may at one time or another observe them is wide indeed. Anyone who sees or hears a ghostly phenomenon is by that very fact psychic. You do not have to be a professional medium to see a ghost, but you do have to possess more than average ESP abilities to tune in on the refined "vibrations" or electromagnetic field of the human personality after it leaves the physical body. There are of course millions of such people in the world, most of them not even aware of their particular ability.

In seeking out some of the houses described in the following pages, keep in mind that a relaxed, open-minded attitude toward the phenomena is helpful. Patience is a must. What might not happen on the first visit might very well occur on a subsequent trip. There is no hard and fast rule concerning a successful ghostly experience, but there is a reasonable likelihood of experiencing something in a haunted house if one is somewhat psychic. If one is psychic to a high degree, chances are that one will at least feel something of the unseen inhabitant of the place. Whenever possible, take photographs using black and white film and a timed exposure—something that the naked eye doesn't see might very well show up on your film.

But even if you don't encounter ghosts or have a psychic experience in the houses described here, you will find them fascinating places. As an adventure in historical research, haunted houses have no equal.

Guide to the Guide

We have taken every step to ensure informational accuracy and the viability of the following excursions. Hopefully the details, phone numbers and specifics in these pages will endure as long as the ghosts, but unfortunately ghosts are more reliable over time than phone numbers, museum hours and admission prices. Before you actually start your adventures in the world of haunted houses, doublecheck your itinerary; a 30 second phone call can sometimes save the cautious traveler infinite amounts of hassle and complication.

How to get there

Each listing has directions guiding travelers to these haunted places—some require a little initiative on the part of the traveler, but all of these places can be found easily.

Nearby accommodations

Between one and four places to stay are listed with each haunted place. You'll find a variety of lodgings in a variety of price ranges—there's something for every kind of traveler. Depending on the remoteness of the haunted site, some accommodations are closer to the actual site than others. Each hotel is listed by name, address and phone number; if the nearest lodging is in a different town than the haunted place, the town is also listed. Next to each phone number, there are dollar signs which indicate the following:

$: The least expensive lodging available nearby—under $100 per night.

$$: The least expensive lodging available nearby—between $100-$150 per night.

$$$: Expensive—over $150 per night.

Key

When you see the following icons associated with a haunted place, it means:

 Museum/Tourist Attraction: These places are open to the public and oriented toward tourism. Guided tours are often available and there will be staff available to answer your questions.

 Public Place: These haunted places are open to the public, but are not tourist attractions (restaurants, hotels, office buildings). You may have take your own initiative to find the hauntings. Be a little cautious about broaching the subject of haunting with the proprietors and staff, and please have respect for their guidelines and rules for public access.

 Outdoor Area: This icon indicates the places listed in this guide that are outdoors and not associated with a building or street.

 Open Seasonally: These places are only open to the public during the summer—specific dates are indicated (where possible) for each.

 Private Places: These buildings are privately owned, and you need permission to enter. You may observe them from the road or street, but don't go any further than that without the express consent of the owners. Many of these buildings are historic landmarks or famous for reasons beside their haunting, so asking permission to look around is not out of the ordinary.

HAUNTED PLACES

in the

UNITED STATES

The San Francisco Ghost Bride

Nob Hill, San Francisco, California

Not far from the Fairmont Hotel (where the popular 1980s television series *Hotel* was taped), on Nob Hill in San Francisco, is a spot many consider haunted. Here on California Street, in front of an ordinary, somewhat aged, apartment house, the ghost of Flora Sommerton walks. Many have seen the girl, dressed in her bridal gown, walk right through living people. She is totally oblivious of them, and they of her. Some years ago a woman (with whom I worked on a number of cases), was riding with a friend up the hill in a cable car. Both saw the strange girl in her bridal gown walking quickly as if trying to get away from something—or someone.

Getting away is exactly what she had been trying to do. Flora Sommerton, a San Francisco debutante, was 18 when she disappeared from her family's Nob Hill mansion one night in 1876. It was a major society scandal at the time: Flora simply refused to marry the young man her parents had picked for her to marry.

Flora never came back, nor was she ever found, despite a vast search and huge reward offered for her return or information leading to her. Years went by and eventually the matter was forgotten. Flora's parents died, and it was not until 1926 that the truth finally came out. That year, Flora died in a flophouse in Butte, Montana, still dressed in her bridal gown.

Ever since, she has been seen walking up Nob Hill desperately trying to escape an unwanted marriage. She appears most often late at night or early in the morning, when there is little traffic.

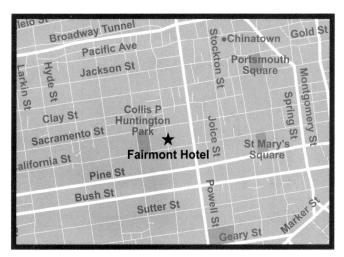

How to get there

The Fairmont Hotel is good place to start, and can be reached by the California Street cable car, on foot or by car. Walk down from there and you may encounter the ghost bride. Nob Hill also borders San Francisco's Chinatown, a great place to explore, shop and eat.

Nearby accommodations

HOLIDAY LODGE AND GARDEN HOTEL
1901 Van Ness Ave.
(415) 776-4469 or (800) 367-8504 $

UNION STREET INN
2229 Union St.
(415) 346-0424 $$

THE FAIRMONT HOTEL
950 Mason St.
(415) 772-5000 or (800) 527-4727 $$$

The Restless Monks of Aetna Springs
Aetna Springs Golf Course
Calistoga, California

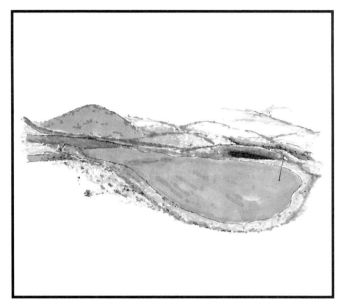

North of San Francisco and the wine-growing Napa Valley lies the Pope Valley—a beautiful, fertile and slightly remote part of Northern California. There are a few notable mineral springs there, including the historic Aetna Springs golf course.

The golf course is the center of an exciting manifestation. In 1963 doctor and amateur photographer Andrew von Salza came to Aetna Springs on holiday. The resort's proprietor owned a stereo camera which was then somewhat of a novelty. Dr. von Salza borrowed it and took two pictures. When the pictures came back from the lab, they showed not just the golf course, but rows of semi-transparent monks, enveloped in flames, walking on the fairway.

Several years later I visited the place in the company of trance medium Sybil Leek, who knew nothing of either the place or Dr. von Salza's amazing photographs. She immediately became very agitated and spoke of a group of monks' elimination by another group—by fire. When I questioned her, she said the leader of the victimized monks was named Jerome.

Inquiries at the California Historical Society yielded

18

little—as far as they knew, there had been no monks this far north. However, a further search produced the answer to this puzzle. At the Hispanic Society Museum in New York I discovered a document detailing problems with a group of monks in the northern part of California. They had complained to the Spanish Crown about the maltreatment of Native American labor in California. Instead of alleviating the problem, the Spanish Crown ordered that Dominicans headquartered at San Francisco eliminate the insurgent monks. The deed was carried out through a deadly act of arson. The leader of the murdered monks was indeed Jerome, and the group was known as the Jeronomite Fathers.

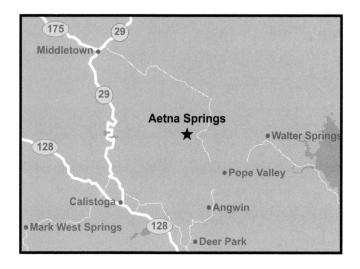

How to get there

Drive up Route 29 from San Francisco past Napa into the Pope Valley, until you reach Calistoga. From there, the Aetna Springs Golf Course is a short drive to the northeast. Call them at (707) 965-2115 for further directions.

Nearby accommodations

DR. WILKINSON'S HOT SPRINGS
1507 Lincoln Ave., Calistoga, CA 94515
(707) 942-4102 $

CALISTOGA SPA HOT SPRINGS
1006 Washington St., Calistoga, CA 94515
(707) 942-6269 $$

COMFORT INN
1865 Lincoln Ave., Calistoga, CA 94515
(707) 942-6269 $$$

The *Queen Mary*
Long Beach, California

Since 1967, the great British ocean liner *Queen Mary* has been safely moored in Long Beach. She is now a museum and a great attraction to visitors from around the world. Stories about ghostly sightings abound, starting with her early years as a ship, through World War II when she carried troops and again later as a luxury liner.

Most of these sightings, however, are what we call psychic imprints from the past, not personalities with unfinished business on their minds. However, there are two cases of bona fide ghosts, and they have never been laid to rest.

In 1966 a young crewman named John Pedder was accidentally crushed to death in doorway #13 during a routine watertight door drill. His ghost has frequently been observed and described in great detail by security guards and various visitors. The sightings of the late Mr. Pedder are remarkably consistent with one another; appearances are usually preceeded by a loud sound, described by one night watchman as "metal rolling quickly toward me."

Another ghost appears in blue-grey overalls in Shaft Alley, the hallway leading to the propeller shafts of the great ship. He has been sighted many times—always in overalls and sporting a long black beard.

The swimming pool has also been the subject of mysterious accounts; many believe it is the ship's most haunted area. The sound of swimmers playing and splashing around has been heard on many occasions when the pool was empty. Sometimes wet footprints appear on the deck, where no one has walked. The most interesting phenomenon in this area, however, is in the dressing "boxes" adjacent to the pool. One dressing room has been identified as a portal for psychic phenomena.

How to get there

The *Queen Mary* is safely docked in Long Beach Harbor, right at the end of highway 710.

Nearby accommodations

WESTCOAST LONGBEACH
700 Queensway Dr.
(310) 435-7676 $

RAMADA INN LONG BEACH
5325 E Pacific Coast Highway
(310) 597-1341 $$

HILTON
2 World Trade Center
(310) 983-3400 $$$

The Ghostly Stagecoach Inn

Thousand Oaks, California

Not far from Ventura, at Thousand Oaks, stands an old stagecoach inn; now run as a museum. Between 1952 and 1965, while in the process of being restored to its original appearance, it also served as a gift shop. The couple that ran the gift shop both had sensed the presence of a female ghost in the structure.

The house has 19 rooms and an imposing columnated frontage, a central balcony and shuttered windows, in the manner of the mid-19th century. The building was moved to a new position to make room for the main road running through here. Nevertheless, its grandeur has not been affected.

The inn was erected because of the Butterfield Mail route, which was projected to go through the Conejo Valley on the way to St. Louis. The Civil War halted this plan, and the routing was changed to traverse the Santa Clara Valley.

I investigated the Stagecoach Inn with Gwen Hinzie and psychic medium Sybil Leek. Up the stairs to the left of the staircase, Sybil noticed one of the particularly haunted rooms. She felt that a man named Pierre Devon was somehow connected with the building. Since the structure was still in a state of disrepair, with construction going on all around us, walking up the stairs was not only a difficult but also somewhat dangerous, for we could not be sure that the wooden structure would not collapse from our weight. We stepped very gingerly. Sybil seemed to know just where to turn, as if she had been there before. Eventually, we ended up in a little room to the left of the stairwell. Sybil complained of being cold all over. The man, Pierre Devon, had been killed in that room, she insisted, sometime between 1882 and 1889.

She did not connect with the reported female ghost. However, several people living in the area claim to have seen a tall stranger—out of the corner of an eye, and never for long. Pungent odors, perfume of a particularly heavy kind, also seem to waft in and out of the structure.

Like many inns, this one may have more undiscovered ghosts hanging onto the spot. Life in 19th century wayside inns did not compare favorably with life in today's Hilton. During the stagecoach days, bandits were active in this area. Some people stopping for a night's rest never woke up to see another day.

How to get there

Take Highway 101 to Highway 23 in Thousand Oaks. The Inn is set back from the junction of the two roads.

Nearby accommodations

Vagabond Inn (Ventura)
756 E. Thompson Blvd. (805) 648-5371 $

Ramada Clocktower Inn (Ventura)
181E. Santa Clara St. (805) 652-0141 $$

Country Inn (Ventura)
298 S. Chestnut St. (805) 653-1434 $$$

Missionary Baptist Church

Thousand Oaks, California

Not far from Thousand Oaks, California stands a simple wooden church called Missionary Baptist Church, on a small bluff overlooking the freeway access road. The church is actually an old dairy barn remodeled first into a theater and later into the present church. (The original owner, a Mr. Goebel, sold it to the Conejo Valley Players, an amateur theatrical group.) There is a large door in front and a smaller one in the rear by which one can now enter. There is also an attic, so low that no one can stand up in it—yet the observed hauntings seem to emanate from the attic. Footsteps above were overheard by some of the Conejo Valley Players, when there was positively no one overhead. (Anyone standing in the attic had to be less than three feet tall.)

The phenomena consisted mainly of a man's footsteps pacing up and down in the attic. At first, no one

24

paid attention, trying to pretend the noise was not real. However, members of the audience began asking what the strange goings-on over their heads meant. Was there another auditorium there? Sometimes it sounded as if heavy objects, such as furniture, were being moved around. There was, of course, nothing of the kind in the attic.

What was once the stage for the Conejo Valley Players is now the altar area. The church minister does not take kindly to psychic phenomena, so a visitor must simply walk into the church—for worship, as it were—and receive such psychic impressions as he or she can without causing any stir.

How to get there

A good combination visit with the Stagecoach Inn, the Baptist Church is also along Highway 101 in Thousand Oaks.

Nearby accommodations

WESTLAKE VILLAGE INN
31943 Agoura Rd. Westlake Village, CA 91361
(818) 889-0230 $

CLARION-POSADA ROYALE
1775 Madera Rd. Simi Valley, CA 93065
(805) 584-6300 $$

MALIBU COUNTRY INN
6506 Westward Beach Rd. Malibu, CA 90265
(310) 457-9622 $$$

The Whaley House

San Diego, California

The Whaley House was originally built in 1857 as a two-story mansion by Thomas Whaley, a San Diego pioneer. It stands at the corner of San Diego Avenue and Harney Street, and is now a museum under the guidance of Wayne Cook; it can be visited during daylight hours. As a matter of fact, thousands of people visit every year—not because it is haunted, but because it is an outstanding example of early American architecture. The Whaley house is a California State Historic Landmark and the oldest brick structure in Southern California.

As well as serving as the Whaley family home, this historic building was also a granary, a store, a school, San Diego's first theater and the county courthouse. It was the epitome of functional luxury and the cultural center of late-19th century San Diego. The house's two stories are connected by a staircase. Downstairs are a parlor, music room, library, and in the annex to the left of the entrance, the former county courthouse. At least one haunting is connected with the courtroom. Upstairs are four bedrooms, tastefully furnished per the period during of the Whaley House's zenith—1860 to 1890.

Numerous witnesses, either visitors or those serving as part-time guides or volunteers, have seen ghosts here. Manifestations include the figure of a woman in the courtroom; sounds of footsteps; upstairs windows opening by themselves despite strong bolts installed so they could be opened only from inside; a man in a frock coat and pantaloons at the top of the stairs; organ music in the courtroom, where there is an organ—though at the time no one was near it and the cover closed; even a ghost dog scurrying down the hall toward the dining room. A black rocking chair upstairs moves of its own volition at times, as if someone were sitting in it. A woman in a green plaid gingham dress has been seated in one of the bedrooms upstairs. People have smelled perfume and cigars. A child ghost has been observed by people working in the house, and a baby has been heard crying. Strange lights, cool breezes and cold spots add to the general atmosphere of haunting. Whaley House is probably one of the most actively haunted mansions in the world today.

How to get there
The Whaley House in Old Town, San Diego is open to visitors most of the day. Guides are available to point out the ghostly sites.

Nearby accommodations

COMFORT INN DOWNTOWN
719 Ash St. (800) 221-2222 $

OLD TOWN INN
4444 Pacific Hwy. (800) 643-3025 $$

HACIENDA HOTEL, OLD TOWN
4041 Harney St. (800) 888-1991 $$$

The Haunted Organ

**Battell Chapel, Yale University
New Haven, Connecticut**

Yale University, in New Haven, Connecticut, is a mainstay of the Ivy League; complete with idyllic quads and ivy-covered buildings. Battell Chapel, located in the "Old Campus" section of the University, is a beautiful building and used extensively within the Yale community for religious services and musical performances of all kinds.

A gentleman I know had regular occasion to be in the chapel and involved with the organ. He became aware of a menacing and melancholic sensation in the building, particularly in the basement and organ chambers. While working there at odd hours late in the night, he was acutely aware of an unpleasant sensation lurking around the next corner.

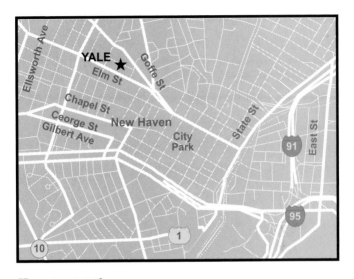

How to get there
Battell Chapel is one of the more important sights at Yale. New Haven can be reached from I-91 from either north or south. Follow signs to Yale University.

Nearby accommodations
HOLIDAY INN AT YALE
30 Whalley Ave.
(203) 777-6221 $

PARK PLAZA HOTEL
155 Temple St.
(203) 865-9034 $$

THE COLONY INN
1157 Chapel St.
(203) 776-1234 $$$

The Curse
of the Dudleys
Dudleytown, Connecticut

About two hours' drive north from New York City, in Litchfield County, lies the ruins of a town called Dudleytown. According to the late medium Ethel Johnson Myers, who lived nearby and visited the often, there are some real ghosts there.

The ruins overlook the village of Cornwall Bridge and used to be a fruitful Native American hunting ground. The village was known for the unusually large owl population living in the oak and chestnut trees—from them the town acquired the nickname of Owlsbury.

In the mid-1800s, English colonists moved into the area; among them were two brothers: Abiel and Barzillai Dudley. The Dudleys farmed the land, prospered and soon the town acquired their name—Dudleytown. But the good fortunes of family and town were not to last. Gradually, settlers moved away, houses crumbled, and the area was once again taken over by trees and animals. By the turn of the century, the town had become a ghost town. There is no rational explanation for this flight from the gentle hills of Connecticut by everyone who came to live there. The real reason for Dudleytown's fate lies elsewhere.

The Cornwall Public Librarian describes Dudleytown as "a tribute to those hardy pioneers who did their best to tame the wild and rocky Connecticut wilderness and failed."

It seems that the Dudley brothers, even though their physical selves moved away, could never let go of their little town in the Connecticut hills.

How to get there

To reach Dudleytown, first go to Cornwall Bridge (easily reached on routes 4 or 7). From town, take Warren Hill Road 1.5 miles southeast. For more information, call the Cornwall Bridge Public Library at (860) 672-6874.

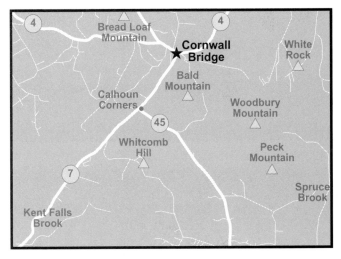

Nearby accommodations

CORNWALL INN
270 Kent Rd. (US 7), Cornwall Bridge, CT 06754
(203) 672-6684 $

FIFE N' DRUM
Rte. 7, Kent, CT 06757
(860) 927-3509 $$

INN ON LAKE WARAMAUG
107 N. Shore Rd, New Preston, CT 06777
(860) 868-0563 $$$

Henry Flagler's Mansion
Palm Beach, Florida

Henry Flagler was Florida's greatest booster, though the eccentric millionaire didn't always please everyone. Since the time of his death, his ghost has been spotted a variety of times at his vast mansion in West Palm Beach.

He made money in grain and oil (he was a co-founder of Standard Oil, the first and largest of the American oil companies), and soon after he was widowed, moved from Cleveland to New York with his small son, where he married his former wife's nurse, Alice.

Flagler discovered St. Augustine on a vacation trip and decided to go into the hotel business, first with the Ponce de Leon Hotel in St. Augustine, and later with the Royal Poinciana in Palm Beach. He "created" St. Augustine, making it into a fashionable resort, and did the same for Palm Beach. Meanwhile Alice became ill and was confined to a mental institution.

In 1895, Henry Flagler went to work to "create" Miami. With Alice out of the way, Flagler met a young singer named Mary Kenan. But both father and son, now grown, were in love with Mary, and it destroyed their relationship. Henry divorced his (second) wife and bribed the Florida legislature to pass a special law to make it possible for him to marry Mary Kenan.

Outraged Floridians forced Henry to leave the state.

He lived with Mary in suburban New York, but the call of Florida was too strong to resist, and he decided to return there. To regain his lost popularity with the people of Florida, Henry decided to do something spectacular: he built a railroad connecting the mainland with the Keys. The railroad, before it was washed away by a storm some 30 years after Flagler's death, extended all the way to Key West. At age 82, Henry was once more a hero.

In 1900, he built "Whitehall" for Mary Kenan. Hailed as the "Taj Mahal of North America", the 55 room mansion was without equal in Florida, and continues to be one of the United States' most lavish homes.

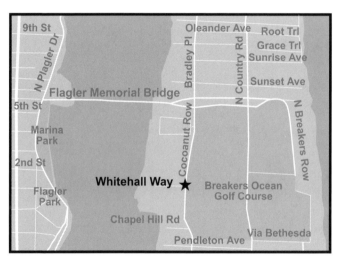

How to get there

The Henry Morrison Flagler Museum sits right in the heart of posh Palm Beach, at the corner of Cocoanut Row and Whitehall Way. It is open from 10 to 5 Tuesday through Saturday, and 12 to 5 Sundays (closed Mondays and holidays). For more information about this historic mansion, you may call the museum at (561) 655-2833.

Nearby accommodations

BEST WESTERN PALM BEACH LAKES
1800 Palm Beach Lakes Blvd.
(561) 683-8810 $$

HIBISCUS HOUSE
501 30th St.
(561) 863-5633 $$

OMNI
1601 Belvedere Rd.
(561) 689-6400 $$$

The Haunted Frigate *Constellation*
Baltimore, Maryland

The proud U.S. Frigate *Constellation*, once a flagship of the American Navy, is tied up at the pier in Baltimore and open to the public as a floating museum. Built in 1797 as the first man-of-war of the United States fleet, the ship was still in commission as · late as World War II. Part of its superstructure has been restored, and the timbers are only partially the original wood, but otherwise nothing has been changed. This is important, since the hauntings would not continue if most or all of the original material had been replaced.

The first ghost is an old sailor by the name of Neil Harvey, who keeps appearing to visitors in his uniform of bygone days. The other two haunting entities were closely associated with each other: Captain Thomas Truxtun and a watch who had fallen asleep on duty and, in the cruel manner of the times, was condemned to death by the captain, who had him strapped to a gun and blown to bits. Captain Truxtun's own feelings of guilt about this execution perhaps caused him to remain aboard.

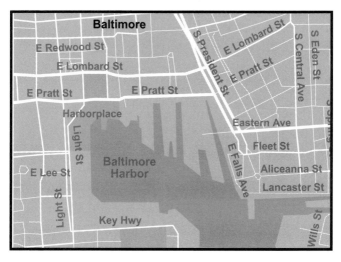

How to get there

The U.S. Frigate *Constellation* can be found at the pier in Baltimore Harbor and can be visited at all times. It is now not only a national landmark but also a museum.

Nearby accommodations

Best Western-East
5625 O'Donnell St.
(410) 633-9500 $$

Hopkins Inn
3404 St. Paul St.
(410) 235-8600 $$

Celie's Waterfront Bed & Breakfast
1714 Thames St.
(410) 522-2323 $$$

The Mary Surratt Tavern
Clinton, Maryland

Thirteen miles south of Washington, in a small town now called Clinton but once known as Surrattville, stands an 18th-century building nowadays used as a museum. Mary Surratt ran it as an inn at a time when the area was a long enough journey from Washington to serve as a way station for those traveling north from the nation's capital. When business fell off, however, Mrs. Surratt leased the tavern to John Lloyd and moved to Washington, where she ran a boardinghouse on H Street between 6th and 7th Streets. But she remained on friendly terms with her successor at the tavern at Surrattville, so that it was possible for her son John Surratt to use it as an occasional meeting place with his friends—including John Wilkes Booth. Those meetings eventually led to the plot to assassinate President Lincoln.

After the murder, Booth escaped on horseback and made straight for the tavern. By prearrangement, he and an associate hid their guns in a cache in the floor of the tavern. Shortly after, he and the associate, David Herald, split up, and John Wilkes Booth continued his journey despite a broken foot. He ended his journey at the infamous Garrett farm, where he was discovered, hiding in the barn, and killed.

The hauntings observed at the tavern include a woman, thought to be the restless spirit of Mary Surratt, whose home it had been. Strange men have been observed sitting on the back stairs when there was no one about but the occupants of the house. Muffled voices of a group of men talking in excited tones have also been reported, and seem to indicate that at the very least an imprint from the past has been preserved at the Surratt Tavern. Many meetings of the conspirators took place in the downstairs part of the building, and when I brought Sybil Leek to the tavern she immediately pointed out the site of the meetings, the place where the guns had been hidden, and, in trance, established communication with the former owner of the tavern, Edwin Booth (reknowned actor and brother of John Wilkes Booth) himself.

Clinton is less than an hour's drive from downtown Washington.

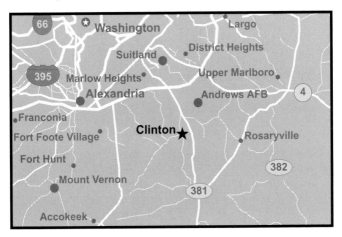

How to get there

Thirteen miles north of Washington, D.C. is the town of Clinton, Maryland. The Surratt Tavern is now a museum and can be visited during regular daytime hours.

Nearby accommodations

ECONO LODGE OLD TOWN
700 N Washington St, Alexandria, VA 22314
(703) 836-5100 $

BEST WESTERN OLD COLONY INN
615 1st St, Alexandria, VA 22314
(703) 739-2222 $$

COLONY SOUTH
7401 Surratts Rd, Clinton, MD 20735
(301) 856-4500 $$$

The Viking Ghosts of Follins Pond

Cape Cod, Massachusetts

A few years ago, I was working with the late British medium Sybil Leek. We were on a visit to Cape Cod to visit some haunted houses—their owners had asked us for our help. I decided to check out some other places where ghostly experiences had been reported in the area; one in particular that originated with the Vikings that landed on Cape Cod many years ago. I did not tell Sybil anything about the reports or the alleged background of the ghosts, I just wanted to see what she might "pick up".

I took her to a relatively obscure body of water in the heart of the northern Cape called Follins Pond. It is a beautiful little lake, surrounded by trees. We crossed the Bass River and made our way to Follins

Pond. Sybil immediately ran to the water's edge, agitated by what she was experiencing there. She described a longboat at the bottom of the pond, and "saw" a number of Norsemen walking around the shore of the little pond.

With a little further investigation, we learned that the Vikings had landed in this area around the year 1000. At that time, the pond was not yet a pond, but a tiny inlet that was still connected to the Atlantic. As time passed, centuries of silt and sand deposited and closed the inlet off from the sea.

How to get there

Take Route 6 to Yarmouth and then north a short way to Route 134. The pond is halfway between Cape Cod Bay and Nantucket Sound.

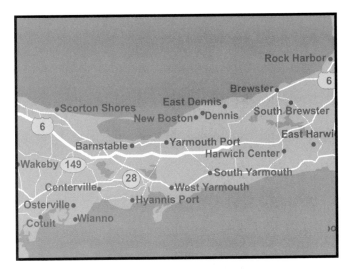

Nearby accommodations

BASS RIVER
891 MA 28, Bass River, MA 02664
(508) 398-2488 $

COLONIAL HOUSE
Old Kings Hwy (M6A), Yarmouth Port, MA 02675
(508) 362-4348 $$

LIBERTY HILL
77 MA 6A, Yarmouth Port, MA 02675
(508) 362-3976 $$$

The Ship Chandler's House

Cohasset, Massachusetts

The solid two-story house at 6 Elm Street in Cohasset, not far from Boston, is now a maritime museum. When it was built in 1760, it was the pride and joy of Samuel Bates, whose family prospered in the ship chandlery business. The house stood by the seashore long after Samuel had presumably gone to his just reward.

Later owners of the property thought a new location in town would be more conducive to tourist visits, so in 1957 they moved the house to a new location. While they were at it, the town decided to fix up some of the old furbishings such as doors and windows, or replace them with new ones. One would think these improvements would please the late Samuel Bates and his descendants.

But all was not well at the "Ship Chandlery and Counting House," as it was formally called once the property was moved inland. Persistent reports of heavy footfalls, as if caused by a substantially built man, were talked about in town, and it was soon clear to one and all in Cohasset that old man Bates wasn't happy.

It came as no surprise to anyone in town that the late Bob Kennedy, the celebrated Boston radio personality, brought me to look into the matter at the Chandlery and find out what was going on.

Mrs. E. Stoddard Marsh, who was then the curator,

and Robert Frost, her associate, had both heard footsteps at various times, and experienced a peculiar cold spot in what had been Mr. Bates's inner office upstairs.

With the help of psychics, both amateur and volunteer, and one professional, Alice McDermott, I was able to establish the cause of the haunting. Samuel Bates, or his ghost, was upset about the house having been moved inland away from the seashore.

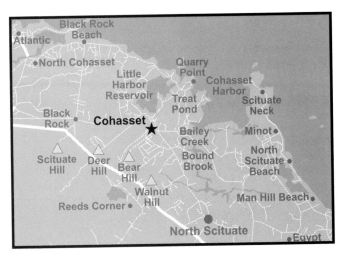

How to get there

The Ship Chandlery and Counting House is administered by the Cohasset Historical Society and open to visitors during the summer. Cohasset is not too far from Boston, at the sea shore, near Quincy. For more specific directions and further information on visiting the museum, you may contact the Cohasset Historical Society at 14 Summer Street, Cohasset, MA 02025, (781) 383-1434.

Nearby accommodations

SUSSE CHALET
800 Morrissey Blvd, Boston, MA 02122
(617) 287-9100 $

HOLIDAY INN-BOSTON/RANDOLPH
1374 N Main St, Randolph, MA 02368
(617) 961-1000 $$

SHERATON-TARA
37 Forbes Rd, Braintree, MA 02184
(617) 848-0600 $$$

The Guthrie Theater
Minneapolis, Minnesota

Looking at the modern Guthrie Theater in Minneapolis, Minnesota, one would never think it could harbor a ghost—except maybe now and then the ghost of Hamlet's father.

A young man named Robert Miller, born in 1951, had come to work as an usher in the theater. At college he had not exactly been successful, and due to a skiing accident also had physical problems. This prevented him from ever skiing again, his greatest pleasure, and soon after he committed suicide by shooting himself in his car.

Several years later, two young employees were spending the night in the theater to monitor the air-conditioning equipment. They were alone, yet someone was playing the piano on stage! When they investigated, they saw a cloudlike figure floating away from the piano. Several ushers working in the theater had also felt his presence or seen smoke-like formations.

An usher working aisle #18, Miller's former beat, was about to leave the theater, as the last one out. He glanced back at the empty theater and there, standing next to the aisle, was Robert Miller's ghost.

A member of the opera troupe connected with the Guthrie saw a strange young man as she was in her car about to drive away from the theater. Her description fit that of Robert Miller exactly. When she challenged him, he vanished instantly.

How to get there

The Guthrie Theater is one of Minneapolis' major cultural attractions and you may want to watch a performance during the season. It is on Vineland Place, in the heart of the city. Ask the usher to take you down aisle 18!

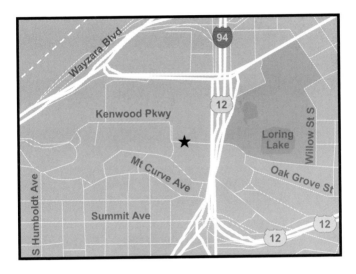

Nearby accommodations

RAMADA INN
2540 N Cleveland Ave.
(612) 636-4597 $$

SHERATON PARK PLACE
1500 Park Place Blvd.
(612) 542-8600 $$

SHERATON METRODOME
1330 Industrial Blvd.
(612) 331-1900 $$

Waverly Mansion
West Point, Mississippi

Built by Colonel George Hampton Young in 1852, this edifice is a splendid example of Greek revival style, and the work of some of the finest artisans the Colonel could persuade to work at West Point. Young died in 1880 and is buried in the family plot near the mansion.

The house stood empty for many years after the family moved on, and was restored from a pretty sad state of disrepair in 1962 by Mr. and Mrs. Robert Shaw of Philadelphia, Mississippi.

But the original builder apparently never quite left, and his presence is sometimes felt, though no apparition has been recorded. However, a little girl ghost, probably a descendant of the original builder, has been seen a number of times.

Waverly Mansion is a national historical landmark, and can be visited, though there is a fee for tourists.

Sylvia Booth Hubbard, chronicler of Mississippi ghost lore, has written about the house and others in that state.

We don't know if the child ghost is still there. But if you, too, hear a little girl calling plaintively for her mother, don't be alarmed.

How to get there

The Mansion is located off Highway 50, between West Point and Columbus, and open daily.

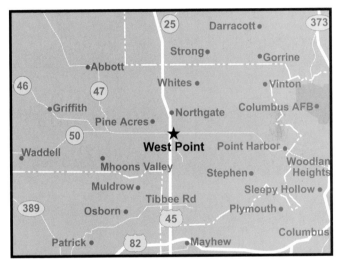

Nearby accommodations

HOLIDAY INN
506 US 45N, Columbus, MS 39701
(601) 328-5202 $

COMFORT INN
1210 US 45N, Columbus, MS 39701
(601) 329-2422 $

Magnolia Hall

Natchez, Mississippi

Built in 1858 by Thomas Henderson, Magnolia Hall is one of the most spectacular mansions built in the area prior to the Civil War. During the War Between the States, much military action took place here, from shelling by gunboats to occupation by Union troops. Operated today by the Natchez Garden Club, the Hall can be visited without difficulty.

The Hall not only boasts some very fine furnishings and antiques, but also the spirit of Thomas Henderson, who apparently still lives there.

Some of the hostesses who take people around the Hall have reported incidents ranging from footsteps in empty rooms to indentations of a head on the pillow of the bed where the late Mr. Henderson slept, to a misty appearance of the owner near the kitchen very late one night.

With so much effort and love poured into a building of this magnitude by its creator, it is not difficult to understand his reluctance to leave it, even in death. Henderson had been paralyzed before his death and could not speak; a local psychic stated that his visits were now his way to communicate.

How to get there

Magnolia Hall is at the corner of Washington and South Pearl Streets in famed Natchez, and open daily from 9 to 5.

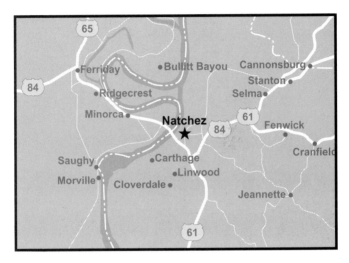

Nearby accommodations

RAVENNASIDE
601 S Union St.
(601) 442-8015 $

NATCHEZ EOLA
110 N Pearl St.
(601) 445-6000 $$

PLEASANT HILL
310 S Pearl St.
(601) 442-7674 $$$

The Living Voices of Virginia City

Virginia City, Nevada

Virginia City was not only the location of the successful television series, "Bonanza", but also a very real historical town. In the 1800s pioneers, adventurers searching for gold, cattle barons and outlaws of the West lived here.

Its once thriving social life is no more, but many of Virginia City's buildings still stand, carefully preserved. Among them is St. Mary's-in-the-Mountains, a church built in 1877 at the height of the Comstock Lode mining fever. Its bell is made of silver from the lode.

Visitors come to Virginia City all the time, partly because of Bonanza, and partly out of genuine historical interest. Several years ago a group of curious students of the psychic visited the church to investigate what had been reported by several witnesses. The witnesses, in no way interested in psychic phenomena, had entered the empty church on a quiet afternoon, only to hear the organ playing music and a faraway sound of garbled voices. But there was no one about, and the organ had long fallen into disuse.

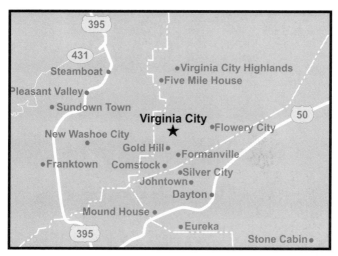

How to get there
St. Mary's is open to visitors during the daytime. Virginia City is a pretty sleepy town, but charming and well preserved. It lies to the west of Carson City.

Nearby accommodations
Best Western Airport Plaza
1981 Terminal Way, Reno, NV 89502
(702) 789-2000 $

Peppermill Hotel Casino
2707 Virginia St, Reno, NV 89502
(702) 826-2121 $$

Hilton Reno
2500 E 2nd St, Reno, NV 89595
(702) 789-2000 $$

The Spy House
Middletown, New Jersey

In June, 1696, Daniel Seabrook, age 26 and a planter by profession, took his inheritance—80 pounds sterling—and bought 202 acres of property from his stepfather, Thomas Whitlock. For 250 years the estate was a plantation in the hands of the Seabrook family who worked the land and sailed their ships from the harbor. The "spy house" is probably one of the finest pieces of Colonial architecture available for inspection in the eastern United States.

Gertrude Neidlinger, the former curator, turned to me for help with the ghosts she felt in the house. Considering the house's history, it's not surprising it has ghosts. There is a woman in white who has been seen coming down from the attic, walking along the hall, entering "the blue and white room". She tucks the covers into a crib or bed, then turns and vanishes. Ms. Neidlinger thought she might be the spirit of Mrs. Seabrook, who lived through the Revolutionary War with relatives on both sides of the political fence.

Upstairs, near the window on the first floor landing, a psychic friend of mine felt a man watching, waiting for someone to come his way. She also felt there was a man named Samuels present, who had committed treason by giving information to the British, and that he was hanged publicly.

But the ghostly lady, the man who was hanged and the man staring out the window onto the bay are not the only ghosts. On the 4th of July, 1975, a group of local boys were in the blue and white room upstairs. Suddenly the sewing machine door opened by itself and the pedals worked without benefit of human feet. One of the boys looked up and in the mirror in the bureau, saw a face with a long beard. Another boy looked down the hall and saw a figure with a tall black hat and a long beard dressed in a period costume.

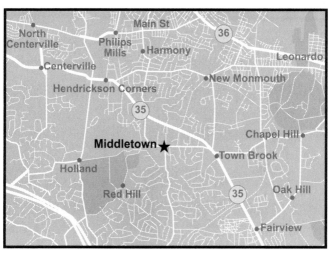

How to get there

Middletown, New Jersey is in Monmouth County. The Spy House is maintained as a museum and can be freely visited.

Nearby accommodations

Wellesley Inn
3215 NJ 35, Hazlet, NJ 07730
(908) 888-2800 $

Ramada Inn
2870 NJ 35, Hazlet, NJ 08830
(908) 264-2400 $$

Oyster Point
146 Bodman Place, Red Bank, NJ 07701
(908) 530-8200 $$$

Ringwood Manor
Ringwood, New Jersey

One of the most interesting haunted houses I have ever visited is only an hour's drive from New York City, in northern New Jersey near Saddle River. It is a manor house known locally as Ringwood Manor, and is considered one of the more important historical houses in New Jersey. Built on land purchased by the Ogden family in 1740, it originally was the home of the owners of a successful iron-smelting furnace.

In 1936, Erskine Hewitt left the estate to the state of New Jersey, and the mansion is now a museum which can be visited daily for a small fee. Not too many visitors come, however, since Ringwood Manor does not get the kind of attention some of the better-publicized national shrines attract.

I visited Ringwood Manor in the company of the late medium Ethel Johnson Meyers to follow up on persistent reports of hauntings in the old mansion. One of the chief witnesses to the ghostly activities was the manor superintendent. He had heard footsteps when there was no one about—footsteps of two different people. Doors that had been shut at night were wide open in the morning, yet no one had been around to open them. The feeling of "presences" in various parts of the house persisted. A local legend says that the ghost of Robert Erskine, the owner of the manor and the iron making operation during the Revolutionary War, walks about with a lantern, but there is no evidence to substantiate this legend.

The center of the hauntings is what was Mrs. bedroom area, but all along the corridors upstairs and downstairs are spots where a sensitive person might experience chills or cold, clammy feelings. I made contact with the surviving personality of Mrs. Erskine, as well as an unhappy servant named Jeremiah.

How to get there

Ringwood Manor is now a museum in Ringwood State Park, near Saddle River. Guides are not shy about talking about ghosts there. You may obtain information about visiting Ringwood through either the State Park (973) 962-7031 or the Friends of Ringwood Manor (973) 962-6118.

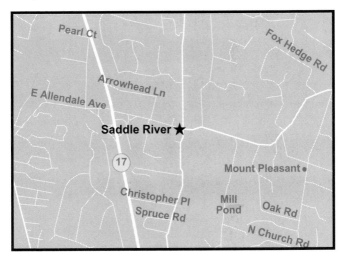

Nearby accommodations

HOWARD JOHNSON
1850 NJ 23 and Ratzer Rd, Wayne, NJ 07470
(201) 696-8050 $

RAMADA INN MAHWAH
180 NJ 17S, Mahwah, NJ 07430
(201) 529-5880 $$

SHERATON CROSSROADS HOTEL
1 International Blvd, Mahwah, NJ 07495
(201) 529-1660 $$$

Garrett Mountain State Park

New Jersey

Passaic County, New Jersey boasts a rather remark-able parkland area, which the Park Commission care-fully oversees from its current headquarters at Lambert Castle. The castle is a 19th-century Great-house built during the Industrial Revolution by a wealthy businessman from England. The park is extensive; entrances have colorful names such as Squirrelwood Road and Weasel Drift Road.

When I first heard about the mysterious happenings in the park, which is relatively untouched woodland on both sides of a central road, I made arrangements to visit it with a clairvoyant. The then director, Ronald F. Dooney, was most sympathetic to our quest and opened the gates for us after dark, when our party—and the ghosts—were the only ones about.

In August of 1976, two young men named Victor Tartaglia and Joe Grosso were driving out of Garrett Mountain Park toward the Weasel Drift Road exit around midnight. The park was supposed to be closed, but one gate was still open, and they were heading for it. They rounded a bend and saw a hunched figure that seemed to be limping. Since they did not want to hit the person, they slowed down until they got closer. Their car lights plainly showed them several things: they could see right through the man; he had an injured arm; and he was wearing a Colonial soldier's uniform. When the lights hit the figure, he turned toward the car, putting out his other arm as if to signal them for help. They were quite close now and realized that the man's body seemed to radiate and his eyes were like "glowing eggs," as they both recalled it. That was too much for them. They stepped on the gas and high-tailed it out of the park.

Since the area was fought over numerous times during the latter part of the 18th century, chances are that a sensitive person could re-experience some of the events, if not actually run into a ghost or two.

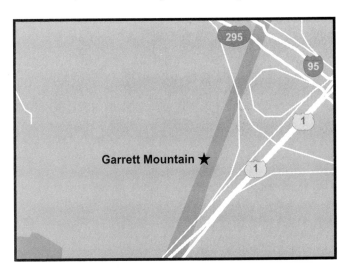

How to get there

Garrett Mountain State Park is open to the public during daylight hours. If you're hoping to run into the Colonial ghost, you may want to drive along the road leading to the Weasel Drift exit.

Nearby accommodations

DAYS INN
850 NJ 120, East Rutherford, NJ 07073
(201) 507-5222 $

HOLIDAY INN
5 Kenney Place, Saddle Brook, NJ 07663
(201) 843-0600 $$

RAMADA INN
265 NJ 3E, Clifton, NJ 07014
(201) 778-6500 $$$

The Deanery, Cathedral of St. John the Divine

New York City

The cathedral church of the Episcopal faith in the eastern United States is St. John the Divine, 1047 Amsterdam Avenue at 110th Street, and it has never been finished. It is huge and impressive, with a smaller building to one side: the Deanery, seat of the cathedral Dean. The largest Cathedral in the world, St. John could comfortably house the Statue of Liberty in its central dome, and it boasts over 150 stained glass windows that depict religious scenes, significant moments in history, and imagery from around the world. The Cathedral is an incredible and powerful place, filled with art treasures, stunning architecture and historic artifacts—worth a visit for a variety of reasons, including its history and more specifically, its haunting.

My late friend, Bishop James Pike, was Dean of this church prior to becoming Bishop of California. During his tenure here, he was frequently disturbed by footsteps where no one was seen walking, and what Jim called "shuffles" on the stairs between the third and fourth floors of the building, which also housed the library and other offices. The third floor was where Pike then lived. When he inquired about the frequent occurrence of these phenomena, he was told that he had in fact encountered the late Bishop Greer. The reason for the late bishop's restlessness was apparently a lost pectoral cross, a very valuable piece given him by Trinity Church, that somehow he lost and never recovered.

I conducted a seance there with the help of Ethel Johnson Meyers, and tried my best to bring peace to the mind of the restless one. It appeared the cross had been shipped to Canada, and no trace of it has been found to this day, and the ghost of Bishop Greer continues to shuffle through the halls of the deanery.

The Cathedral is open daily from 7 am to 6 pm, and there are services at least three times a day, seven days a week. For more information, call (212) 316-7540.

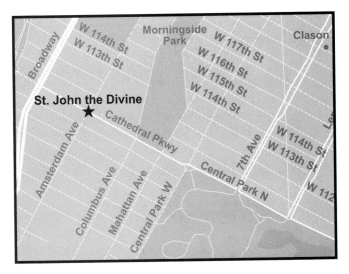

How to get there

St. John the Divine, the great Episcopal Cathedral at Amsterdam Avenue and 110th Street is nearly always open to the public. The house called the Deanery is next to the so-called bishop's house, to the right of the main church. The third floor of the building is the haunted area.

Nearby accommodations

THE FRANKLIN
164 E 87th St.
(212) 369-1000 $$$

HOTEL BEACON
2130 Broadway
(212) 787-1100 $$$

WYNDHAM
42 W 58th St.
(212) 753-3500 $$$

The Conference House
Staten Island, New York

Peace conferences may go on for years and years without tangible results—so it is refreshing to remember that a peace conference on Staten Island between Lord Howe, the British commander in America, and a Congressional committee consisting of Benjamin Franklin, John Adams and Edward Rutledge lasted but a single day: September 11, 1776, to be exact.

Lord Howe outlined his plan for a settlement, explaining that it was futile for the Americans to carry on the war and that the British were willing to offer peace with honor. Of course, any settlement would involve the colonies' remaining under British rule. The three envoys listened in polite silence, after which Benjamin Franklin informed Lord Howe that the Declaration of Independence had already been signed on July 4, 1776, and that they would never go back under British rule.

According to local legends, a young Captain had jilted his fiancee and she died of a broken heart in the house. As a result, strange noises including murmurs, sighs, moans and pleas of an unseen voice have been reported in the house Since the mid-19th century. According to the old Staten Island newspaper The Transcript, the phenomena were heard by workmen during the restoration of the house after it became a museum.

The caretaker admitted hearing heavy footsteps upstairs at times, which sounded to her like those of a man wearing heavy boots with spurs. She claims to have seen a man run up the stairs toward a girl waiting on the first landing. One afternoon, as she dusted the room on the left of the ground floor, she put her hand "right through" a British soldier! Once, her daughter from South Carolina came to visit and insisted on staying upstairs in the haunted rooms. That night the daughter allegedly heard a man's laughter, followed by a woman's laughter, then a shriek. According to the caretaker, this happens at regular intervals.

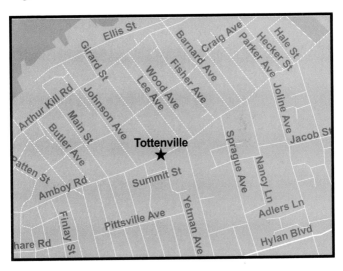

How to get there

Take the ferry at the southern tip of Manhattan to Staten Island, then drive down to Tottenville and ask for the house, which is also known as Bentley Manor. Daytime visits are possible, as the house is maintained as a museum.

Nearby accommodations

BUDGET MOTOR LODGE
350 US 9N, Woodbridge, NJ 07095
(908) 636-4000 $

RARITAN INN
3050 Woodbridge Ave, Edison, NJ 08837
(908) 661-1000 $$

HILTON
120 Wood Ave S, Iselin, NJ 08830
(908) 494-6200 $$$

The Morris-Jumel Mansion

New York City

The Morris-Jumel Mansion in Washington Heights, Manhattan, at the corner of 160th Street and Edgecombe Avenue. Built at the highest spot of Manhattan (originally called Harlem Heights), the mansion was erected by British-born Colonel Roger Morris. In 1776, during the Revolutionary War, General George Washington made it his headquarters during the battle of Long Island. Later on, when the fortunes of war changed, the British moved in again, and General Sir Henry Clinton stayed at the mansion. From then on the career of this magnificent building was somewhat checkered. At one point it served as an ordinary tavern called Calumet Hall. One day in 1810, a French wine merchant by the name of Stephen Jumel, recently arrived on these shores, and his ambitious American-born wife passed by and decided on the spot to buy the place. At that time the property included 35 surrounding acres. Madame Jumel immediately refurbished and renovated the place and it soon became one of the showplaces of New York City.

It was on the balcony on January 19, 1964 that a small group of school children saw the ghost of Madame Jumel. It happened while they were waiting to be let into the building. They had arrived a little early and were becoming restless, when one of the children pointed to the balcony where a lady in a flimsy violet-colored gown had just appeared. "Shush!" she said to the children, trying to calm them down. After that she receded into the room behind the balcony. It never occurred to the children until later that she had never opened the doors, but simply vanished through them. When the curator arrived to let them in, they complained that they could have been in the house much sooner, and why didn't the lady on the balcony open up for them? Needless to say, there was no lady on the balcony, as far as the curator was concerned. But she soon realized that she was presiding over a much-haunted house.

Subsequent curators have been told to downplay the ghosts, out of fear that rowdy elements might want to be difficult on Halloween. That, at least, is their excuse, but the ghosts are still very much in residence.

How to get there

Located at 65 Jumel Terrace, a short two-block street running parallel to Broadway between 160th and 162nd Streets on the Upper Westside of Manhattan, the mansion is open to visitors Wednesday through Sunday, 10 am to 4 pm. Admission for adults is $3, and Students and Seniors get in for $2.

Nearby accommodations

THE FRANKLIN
164 E 87th St.   (212) 369-1000 $$$

HOTEL BEACON
2130 Broadway   (212) 787-1100 $$$

WYNDHAM
42 W 58th St.   (212) 753-3500 $$$

The Old Merchant's House

New York City

Surrounded by old houses, some in a sad state of disrepair, the Old Merchant's House at 29 East 4th Street, Manhattan, not far from the infamous Bowery, stands out like a jewel. The house became the property of Seabury Tredwell, a wealthy merchant in the hardware business, as soon as it was completed by its builder. At the time the house had a garden, and with the river not too far away, it was possible to approach the house on the East River, walk up the slanting acreage, which was then largely open, and visit the house. Research has indicated that secret passageways existed between many of the houses in the area and the river, perhaps remnants of the Revolutionary period when escape from danger made such precautions advisable.

The ghostly phenomena in the house center around Tredwell's three daughters, Phoebe, Sarah and

Gertrude. According to tradition, Mr. Tredwell did not take kindly to any suitor who seemed to want to marry his daughters for their financial status.

The main manifestations occurred in the kitchen in the rear of the house, but Gertrude's bedroom also has a presence in it from time to time. The ghost is that of a small, elegant woman dressed in the finery of the mid-19th century. It's very likely this is Gertrude herself, since according to my late psychic friend Ethel Johnson Meyers, it was she who died tragically here. There had been an unwanted baby, followed by her family's disapproval. That this can be proven objectively is doubtful, but a presence has been observed in the Old Merchant's House by several reliable witnesses, and no attempt has been made to exorcise her, since after all, this was her home. There is a fascinating trapdoor on one of the upper floors, connected perhaps with secret rendezvous between Gertrude and her gentleman friend outside the house.

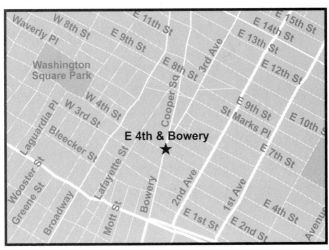

How to get there

The house is at 29 East 4th Street, on the Lower Eastside of Manhattan, and is usually open to the public daily to 4 p.m. Visitors are free to go upstairs and into the cellar. The ghost of Gertrude, however, is still very much in residence.

Nearby accommodations

INN AT IRVING PLACE
56 Irving Place   (212) 533-4600 $$$

STANFORD
43 W 32nd St.   (212) 563-1480 $$

SOUTHGATE TOWER SUITE
371 Seventh Ave.   (212) 563-1800 $$$

The Sonnenberg Mansion

New York City

A magnificent old five-story mansion at 19 Irving Place on New York City's Gramercy Park, the Sonnenberg Mansion was built in the Federal style during the first half of the 19th century.

As time went on, the building changed hands, until some 30 years or so ago it quietly passed into the hands of the very colorful and justly famous theatrical publicist, Ben Sonnenberg. He cherished the mansion and lavished money and effort on it so that it became known as "the Sonnenberg mansion."

But then Sonnenberg died. It had been his last wish to be buried on the grounds of his beloved residence. This was illegal, so the matter had to be dealt with prudently and quietly. Mr. Sonnenberg's earthly remains found their final resting place underneath the bushes on the side of the building facing directly onto Gramercy Park. Which exact bush he was under remained forever a secret.

The building was put up for sale, and the contents

auctioned off separately, thus destroying the integrity of house and furnishings Sonnenberg had spent so many years and so much money to develop. The house stood empty, and naked as some of the ladies of the stage fancied by Sonnenberg must have been at various times in the upper chambers.

Meanwhile, the house was in the care of a young couple who occupied a small flat at the rear in what must once have been the servants' quarters. The husband contacted me about some strange happenings. An attractive woman had appeared on the staircase and then disappeared suddenly, at a time when only he and his wife were about. There were also footsteps and doors being opened and shut by unseen hands.

Currently the mansion is the property of former fashion designer Richard Tyler, who has his offices there, and should not be confused with the Sonnenberg Gardens in upstate New York.

How to get there

The Sonnenberg Mansion, at 19 Irving Place in Gramercy Park, Manhattan, is privately owned. Any enterprising tourist can find an excuse to drop in for a second or two, as it is used as an office building.

Nearby accommodations

INN AT IRVING PLACE
56 Irving Place (212) 533-4600 $$$

STANFORD
43 W 32nd St. (212) 563-1480 $$

GRAMERCY PARK HOTEL
2 Lexington Ave. (212) 475-4320 $$$

The Dorm
with a Ghostly Past
NYU Law School, New York City

Until a few years ago, the Cafe Bizarre (a cafe and bar) could be found on the corner of 3rd Street and Sullivan. Before it was a cafe, the building was part of Aaron Burr's private stables, and on a few separate occasions, the ghost of Aaron Burr has been spotted in and around the cafe.

A young woman named Alice McDermott was having a drink with some friends one night—she looked up from her conversation and saw a strange man, dressed in 18th century-style clothing peering at her from the balcony above. Her account is consistent with those of Rick Allmen, the former owner of the cafe.

Subsequently, I conducted a seance there with the help of medium Sybil Leek, and Burr's ghost spoke through her. He complained bitterly about the injustices of history on his reputation, lamented his exile in France and spoke of his daughter Theodosia, who died in a storm at sea. It was clear that the former Vice-President had no intention of leaving his stable.

A few years ago, however, the building was razed and a much larger building was erected on the site. Today, the D'Agostino Residence Hall, which is part of the NYU Law School, is still the home of the ghost of Aaron Burr. A ghost, unless exorcised from a place, will remain attached to the physical space.

The new address is 110 West 3rd Street, and can be reached by phone at (212) 998-6502.

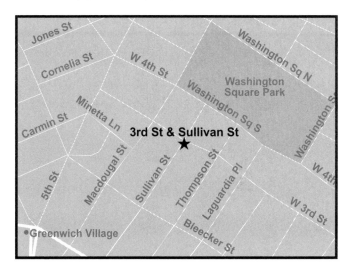

How to get there

Get off the subway at Bleecker, Broadway/Lafayette or West 4th/Washington Square. NYU Law School borders the south end of Washington Square Park.

Nearby accommodations

Inn at Irving Place
56 Irving Place
(212) 533-4600 $$$

Stanford
43 W 32nd St.
(212) 563-1480 $$

Gramercy Park Hotel
2 Lexington Ave.
(212) 475-4320 $$$

St. Mark's-in-the-Bowery

New York City

St. Mark's, a Dutch Reformed church, is one of the most famous landmarks in New York City. It was built in 1799 on the site of an earlier chapel extant during the term of Peter Stuyvesant, governor of New York in 1660. Stuyvesant, who became the legendary Father Knickerbocker, is buried in the crypt. The last member of his family died in 1953 and then the crypt was sealed. One can see the crypts from across the street, as they are half underground and half above-ground, making the churchyard of St. Mark's a unique sight.

Built along neo-classical lines, the church and its cemetery are surrounded by a cast iron fence. The church is open most of the time, though one should look at its schedule of events to see when visitors are permitted, since various concerts and meetings also occur in the church.

St. Mark's boasts three known ghosts. First there is a female parishioner who has been observed by reputable witnesses in the middle of the nave, staring at the altar. She has been described as a Victorian woman, very pale and apparently unhappy. Another ghost has been observed on the balcony near the magnificent organ. Several organists have had the uncanny feeling of being observed by someone they could not see. One of the men working in the church reported hearing footsteps coming up to the organ loft. He assumed that the organist had come to work early and got ready to welcome him, when to his surprise the footsteps stopped and total silence fell. Needless to say, he did not see any organist. Finally, a man walking with a cane has been heard, and it is thought that the limping ghost is none other than Peter Stuyvesant himself, who had a wooden leg and used a cane.

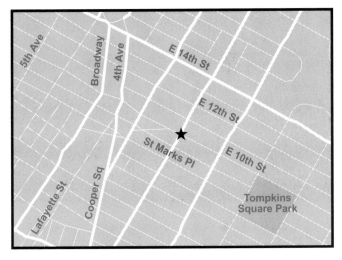

How to get there

Located at the corner of Second Avenue and 10th Street at 131 E 10th, St. Marks is easy to reach by bus or subway, with a short walk from either the Eastside IRT subway stop at Astor Place or the BMT stop at 8th Street.

Nearby accommodations

INN AT IRVING PLACE
56 Irving Place   (212) 533-4600 $$$

STANFORD
43 W 32nd St.   (212) 563-1480 $$

SOUTHGATE TOWER SUITE
371 Seventh Ave.   (212) 563-1800 $$$

The Church of the Ascension

New York City

The Church of the Ascension, on 5th Avenue and 10th Street is one of New York's most beautiful churches The altar painting commissioned by the vestry is by the famous painter John LaFarge. Unfortunately its heavy lead paint caused the painting to fall on several occasions, which led to the accusation by the city fathers that the late LaFarge had not properly designed the scaffolding for the painting.

The fall of the heavy altar painting seems to have caused the painter to remain earthbound; he was seen by several witnesses around the corner, in an artists' apartment and studio house modeled after a similar building in Paris. Sadly, that wonderful Victorian building was torn down and replaced by the

Peter Warren apartment house, which bears the number 45 West 10th Street. While the old studio building was still standing, several tenants in La Farge's former studio had encounters with him and a woman who accompanied him, looking through people's drawers for something, and dissolving into thin air when challenged.

That "something" turned out to be LaFarge's original plans for the scaffolding, in order to clear his good name. Whether LaFarge is still haunting the building at that same spot is hard to tell, but although the painting has not fallen again, there have been several ghostly sightings at the church.

How to get there

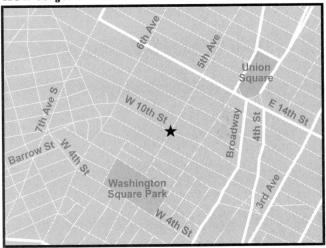

Buses southbound on Fifth Avenue will leave you practically at the church door, or any subway that stops at Union Square would leave you just a few blocks north of the Church of the Ascension.

Nearby accommodations

INN AT IRVING PLACE
56 Irving Place
(212) 533-4600 $$$

STANFORD
43 W 32nd St.
(212) 563-1480 $$

SOUTHGATE TOWER SUITE
371 Seventh Ave.
(212) 563-1800 $$$

The Ghost in the Bar

New York City

There is an Italian restaurant at on west 56th Street, near Sixth Avenue, called Il Brunello: a fairly typical little Italian bistro. Many years ago, however, it was a bar called DaVinci's, where many a midtown executive would go to wind down with a drink after a long day at work.

It was in that period, in the 1950s, when a particular advertising exec, who was a frequent guest at the bar, took to drinking regularly and heavily. Eventually, the DaVinci bar became his home away from home, and there were more than a few times that the bartender had to cut him off, because he had simply had a few too many.

When he died, he apparently never quite left his favorite bar and hangout. Soon after his death, the bartenders would spot glasses on the bar half filled with Martinis, after the bar had been shut tight for the night. Advertising slogans appeared mysteriously on the wall when no one was in the place.

I held a seance there with the late medium Ethel Johnson Meyers, to try to persuade the advertising man to leave for a better place: which he refused to do, but when the medium came out of deep trance, she was visibly drunk!

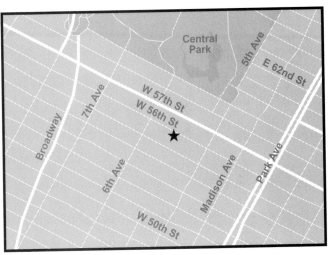

How to get there

Call and make a reservation at Il Brunello, (212) 247-2779, if you want check it out for yourself. They're open for dinner until ten or ten-thirty, seven nights a week. The restaurant can be found at 56 W 56th St. Get off the subway on the west side at Columbus Circle, or on the east side at 59th and Lexington.

Nearby accommodations

STANFORD
43 W 32nd St.
(212) 563-1480 $$

SOUTHGATE TOWER SUITE
371 Seventh Ave.
(212) 563-1800 $$$

WYNDHAM
42 W 58th St.
(212) 753-3500 $$$

The Amityville Horror House

Amityville, New York

Millions of people are familiar with the DeFeo murders that took place in the now infamous house on Ocean Avenue in Amityville, Long Island. It was quite obvious when we came to the house (with trance medium, the late Ethel Johnson Meyers) that the haunting here was not a traditional "ghost story" or related to the multiple murders. It focused on a single, angry entity on whose burial ground the house stood, and nothing more: a Native American chief whose tomb had been violated around the turn of the century, when the rains exposed his skeleton and a youngster broke off the skull.

All the disturbances in that house since—and in the future, one presumes—stem from this fact.. The terrible events in the house have perhaps overshadowed the earlier misdeed, but it is my conviction that the DeFeo crimes were due to possession of young Ronald DeFeo by the avenging Chief, and not by his own volition at all. When I interviewed the young man in his cell at Dannemora Maximum Security

Prison, the Chief did not allow me to put the young man into hypnotic trance (so he could retrace his steps on the night of the murders).

On the night of Friday, November 13, 1974, six members of the DeFeo family were brutally murdered in their beds in one of the most horrifying and bizarre mass murders of recent memory.

The lone survivor of the crime, Ronald DeFeo, Jr., who had initially notified police, was soon after arrested and formally charged with the slayings. But there are aspects to the case that have never been satisfactorily resolved.

Amityville is privately owned and access depends knowing someone who might help you, but you can look at the place from the outside and soak in the atmosphere without disturbing anyone.

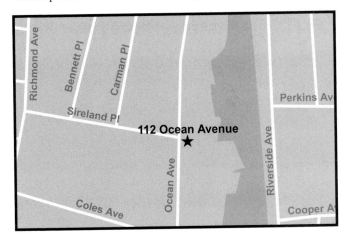

How to get there

Amityville can be reached from New York City via the Long Island Expressway. When you see the exit sign for Amityville, turn off the expressway to the right and go to the end of the road, almost to the Long Island Sound. Ocean Avenue is easy to find; the house is #112.

Nearby accommodations

RAMADA INN LIMITED
8030 Jericho Turnpike, Woodbury, NY 11797
(516) 921-8500 $

MELVILLE MARRIOTT
1350 Old Walt Whitman Road, Melville, NY 11747
(516) 423-1600 $$

HILTON
598 Broad Hollow Rd, Melville, NY 11747
(516) 845-1000 $$$

Church of Christ Rectory

Poughkeepsie, New York

Bishop James Pike, one-time Bishop of California and the author of a number of remarkable books, was no stranger to psychic phenomena. During my work with him, I got to know the Church rectory at Poughkeepsie pretty well. In 1947 Pike was offered the position of rector, and spent several years there.

The Church of Christ is a large, beautiful, Episcopal church. The altar is somewhat "high church," that is, similar to Roman Catholic style. The church exterior and attached rectory remain turn-of-the-century. There is also a small library between the rectory and the church.

What occurred during the two and a half years of Pike's residency at Poughkeepsie was not unusual, as hauntings go. To him it was merely puzzling, and he made no attempt to follow up on it as I did when I brought a medium to the scene.

Pike had taken over his position at Poughkeepsie, replacing an elderly rector with diametrically opposed views in church matters. The former rector had died shortly afterward. Pike soon found that his altar candles were being blown out, doors shut of their own volition, and objects overhead would move—or seem to—when in fact they did not. All the noises and disturbances did not particularly upset Bishop Pike. However, on one occasion he found himself faced with a bat flying madly about in the library. Knowing that there was no way in or out of the library except by the door he had just opened, he immediately closed the door again and went to look for an instrument with which to capture the bat. When he returned and cautiously opened the door to the library, the bat had disappeared.

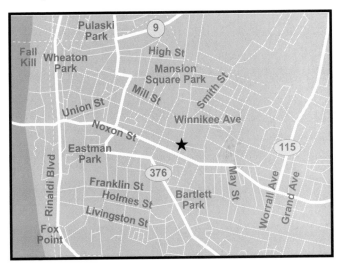

How to get there

The church can be visited during business hours; the rectory is attached to it. Access to the rectory should be possible, as not too many tourists come here. Poughkeepsie can be reached from New York City in about an hour and a half, driving up the Thruway (I-95) or take a train from Grand Central Station in Manhattan. Take the Noxon Road exit and follow Noxon to Route 55.

Nearby accommodations

DAYS INN
62 Haight Ave. (914) 454-1010 $

HOLIDAY INN EXPRESS
US 9 & Sharon Dr. (914) 473-1151 $$

INN AT THE FALLS
50 Red Oaks Mill Rd. (914) 462-5770 $$$

Ghosts in the Barracks

West Point, New York

Just before the outbreak of the second World War, four cadets at the United States Military Academy saw the apparition of a soldier in 18th-century cavalry uniform, and according to the witnesses, the apparition seemed luminous and shimmering. Apparently, the ghost materialized out of the wall and a closet in room 4714, and on one occasion also from the middle of the floor.

As soon as the publicity drew the attention of the guiding spirits (of the military kind) to such incidents, room 4714 was emptied of its human inhabitants. The room itself was then declared off-limits to one and all. One captain, however, was willing to discuss it intelligently. "There is no doubt about it at all," he said, "the room grew unnaturally cold." Two weeks before, he and another upperclassman spent a night sleeping in the room, their beds separated by a partition. At about 2:00 a.m. his roommate began to shout. The captain jumped from his bed and rounded the partition, but could not see anything out of the ordinary. He did feel, however, an icy cold for which there was no rational explanation.

Two plebes who occupied room 4714 before them also had a ghostly encounter at the same spot. The second time the apparition walked out of a bureau that stood in the middle of the floor. The captain heard the plebes shout, and ran into the room. One of the cadets was able to furnish a drawing of the apparition: the face of a man with a drooping mustache and a high old-fashioned cap surmounted by a feather. The uniform is that of a cavalry man of about 200 years ago.

Another cadet was taking a shower prior to moving into the haunted room, and on leaving the shower noticed his bathrobe swinging back and forth on the hook. Since the door and window were closed, there could be no breeze causing the robe to move. The building in which this occurred stands on old grounds; an earlier barracks had long since been demolished. Could it be that the ghostly cavalry man might have died there and was unable to adjust to his new surroundings?

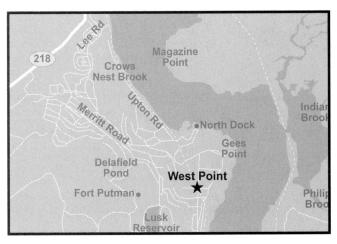

How to get there

West Point Military Academy is just north of Peekskill in upstate New York. The academy is open to visitors in the daytime, and has tour guides available. Once there, try to find the building that contains room 4714. Company G-4 is quartered there; enlist the help of a sympathetic student to show you to room 4714.

Nearby accommodations

THAYER
Inside S Gate, West Point US Military Academy, NY 10996
(914) 446-4731 $$

HUDSON HOUSE
2 Main St, Cold Spring, NY 10516
(914) 265-9355 $$$

THE BIRD & BOTTLE
Old Albany Post Rd (US 9), Garrison, NY 10524
(914) 424-3000 $$$

Raynham Hall

Oyster Bay, New York

There are actually two houses called Raynham Hall: the older one in England was the ancestral seat of the Townsend family, is located in Norfolk and not open to tourists. There, a photographer accidentally obtained a photograph of the resident ghost, Lady Dorothy Walpole, which Life Magazine published in 1937. The other Raynham Hall, in Oyster Bay, Long Island, was purchased by colonists Samuel & Sarah Townsend in the 1770's and named after his family's ancestral home in Norfolk. They had eight children, and their home quickly became a centerpoint in Oyster Bay— Samuel was the Town Clerk and Justice of the Peace, as well as the proprietor of a small general store, in charge of a fleet of trading sloops and a farmer.

A lovely example of colonial saltbox architecture, Raynham Hall was remodeled in 1851 by Solomon Townsend II, Samuel and Sarah's grandson. He was a wealthy New York merchant, and he continued the Raynham Hall's tradition of style and history.

The ghost here is associated with the British who were quartered in the house during the Revolutionary war. The house is famous for housing the Queens Rangers, a Loyalist regiment led by Lieutenant Colonel John Graves Simcoe. Apparently, it was a member of the Townsend family that led to the capture of Loyalist

Major Andre (who also allegedly had an affair with Sally Townsend, one of the original eight Townsend children).

Locals suggest the ghost is Major Andre, but he did not die here. Phenomena reported are footsteps and the feeling of unseen presences. If anyone could be the ghost, it might be the unhappy Sally; not only was she jilted by the British officer, but her father also broke with her over the affair. The museum guides today are more than willing to discuss the hauntings at Raynham Hall, so don't hesitate to ask them questions.

The house is found at 20 West Main Street, Oyster Bay, New York 11771, and can be reached by phone (516) 922-6808. Located near the heart of downtown, Raynham Hall is open to the public Tuesday-Sunday year round, from 1pm to 5pm (Closed on New Year's, Thanksgiving and Christmas). Admission for adults is $2, Seniors & Students get in for $1 and children under 7 get in free of charge.

How to get there
Take exit 41N off the Long Island Expressway 495 or exit 35N off the Northern State Parkway, to Route 106 North into Oyster Bay. Take a left onto Main Street and park. You can also take the Long Island Railroad from Manhattan into the center of town.

Nearby accommodations
RAMADA INN LIMITED
8030 Jericho Turnpike, Woodbury, NY 11797
(516) 921-8500 $$

HUNTINGTON COUNTRY INN
270 W Jericho Turnpike, Huntington, NY 11746
(516) 421-3900 $$

EAST NORWICH INN
6321 Northern Blvd, East Norwich, NY 11372
(516) 922-1500 $$$

The Ghosts at Gettysburg

Gettysburg, Pennsylvania

Gettysburg, Pennsylvania is the site of one of the most significant battles of the Civil War, and later, of Lincoln's infamous address. At one point in his speech, President Lincoln said that "these dead shall not have dies in vain", an interesting prelude to the ghosts that continue to haunt the battlefield.

On the battlefield, there is a spot called Little Round Top, where one of the bloodiest engagements of the war took place. Today, you will find a historical monument and memorials to the soldiers who died there. There have been a number of sightings of a phantom soldier wandering this area—he appears to be looking for his regiment and he is clearly not cognizant that he has been killed in battle.

Another ghostly tale in this area takes places in an old inn called the Graeffenburg, which stands next to the battlefield. A young woman named Helen Forrest was born there, and her family ran the small tourist hotel. Even as a young girl, Helen recalls hearing a woman's voice in her room when no one was present. The ghost would sing, open windows, move furniture and leave a faint lilac scent in room 32. Helen's father refused to let anyone stay in that room—a tradition that has, for the most part, continued to this day, even though Mr. Forrest has long since passed.

Helen returned to the inn when she was in her thirties, and requested room 32 for the night. The manager told her that two of the previous managers had stayed in the room, and both were smothered to death while they slept. Helen decided to stay in the room anyway. In the middle of the night, she awakened from a deep sleep, to find herself being shaken violently awake. She leapt out of bed to find the room ablaze and a small old woman in a nightgown gazing at her and standing amidst the flames. The room was gutted, but has since been restored and is open to visitors.

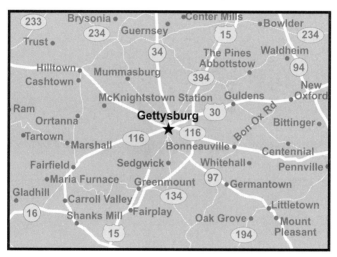

How to get there

Gettysburg is most easily reached on Interstate 15—take the business loop into the center of town, where you will find the tourist information center in the center of town, on Baltimore Street. They will be able to direct you to the above places and the multitudes of other interesting historic places in the area.

Nearby accommodations

COLLEGE INN
345 Carlisle St. (717) 334-6731 $

GASLIGHT
33 East Middle St. (717) 337-9100 $$

BRAFFERTON
44 York St. (717) 337-9100 $$$

The Haunted Church

Millvale, Pennsylvania

About five miles north of Pittsburgh, in the small town of Millvale, by the Allegheny River, stands an imposing stone church built at the turn of the last century. Positioned on a bluff over the river, it seems somewhat out of place for such a small town. A school and rectory are attached to the building, and there is an air of clean efficiency about the entire complex. It is a Roman Catholic church, and the priests are of Slavic background. Thus there is a Slavic cast to the ritual and the atmosphere inside the church. The church is very large, the altar is framed by original paintings by Maxim Hvatka, the celebrated Slavic artist who worked in the early part of this century and died several years ago. Near the altar is a large "eternal light"—an enclosed candle protected from drafts or other interference. Much of the phenomenon centers in this area and includes the blowing out of the eternal light by unknown causes.

Although church administrators do not exactly cherish the notion that they have a ghost, there have been a number of witnesses who have seen a figure pass by the altar. Hvatka himself saw the ghostly apparition while working on his frescoes. Chills which could not be accounted for were also noted in the immediate area of the eternal light.

Nothing connected with the present-day church would account for the apparition of a figure at the altar. However, prior to the erection of the present church, a wooden church had occupied the same spot. Father Ranzinger, who built the wooden church, devoted most of his life to that church and its flock. One night, the church went up in flames and Father Ranzinger's life's work was destroyed. I suspect it is his ghost that has been seen.

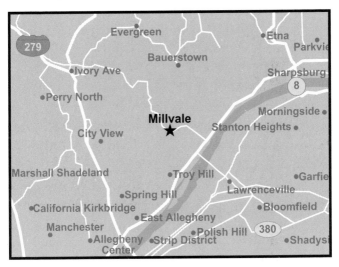

How to get there

Millvale is about 5 miles from Pittsburgh near the Allegheny River. The church stands on a bluff overlooking the river.

Nearby accommodations

BEST WESTERN PARKWAY CENTER INN
875 Greentree Rd, Pittsburgh, PA 15220
(412) 922-7070 $$

THE PRIORY
614 Pressley St, Pittsburgh, PA 15222
(412) 231-3338 $$

DOUBLETREE
1000 Penn Ave, Pittsburgh, PA 15222

The Logan Inn
New Hope, Pennsylvania

When I decided to spend a quiet weekend to celebrate my birthday at the picturesque Logan Inn in New Hope, Pennsylvania, I had no idea that I was not only going to sleep in a haunted bedroom, but also get two ghosts for the price of one! The other ghost I encountered at the Black Bass Inn, in a nearby town.

The lady who communicated with my companion and myself in the darkness of the silent January night, via a flickering candle in room #6, provided a heartwarming experience and one I can only hope helped the restless one get a better sense of still belonging to the house. Mrs. Gwen Davis, the proprietor, assured me that the ghost is the mother of a former owner, who simply liked the place so much she never left.

A far cry from the chain rattling ghosts of medieval castles, the "stay-behind" (as I have come to call gentle spirits who just never left their old homes because they were so very strongly attached to them), the ghostly lady at the Logan Inn is warm and loving.

The inn itself, ghost room or not, has a friendly spirit all its own. It's as charming a place as you can find in New Hope, Pennsylvania, which is a pretty charming little town. New Hope is just over the New Jersey line, on the Delaware Canal. The haunted room is number 6, though the ghost has also been seen walking in the hallways and on the stairs.

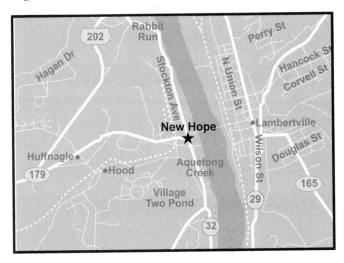

How to get there

From New York and other points north and east, you should take the New Jersey Turnpike to I-78 West. From there, find I-287 South to Route 202 South and then over the Delaware River Toll Bridge. Take your first right onto Route 32 South. The Logan Inn is on Ferry Street in New Hope.

From Philadelphia and other points south and west, take I-95 North to the New Hope Exit (31). Make a left at the stop sign onto Taylorsville Road. Continue approximately 5 miles on Taylorsville Road. At the stop sign, turn left onto Route 32 North (River Road), and follow it for approximately four miles into New Hope.

Nearby accommodations

THE LOGAN INN
#10 W Ferry Street.
(215) 862-2300 $$$

INN AT PHILLIPS MILL
2590 N River Road, New Hope, PA 18938
(215) 862-2984 $

CENTRE BRIDGE
2998 N River Road, New Hope, PA 18938
(215) 862-9139 $$

The Black Bass Inn

Lumberville, Pennsylvania

The Black Bass Inn is an 18th-century pub and hotel right on the Delaware Canal. The place is filled with English antiques of the period and portraits of Kings Charles I and II and James II, proving that this at one time was indeed a Loyalist stronghold.

The story here concerned the ghost of a young man who made his living as a canal boatsman. Today, the canal is merely a curiosity for tourists, but in the 19th century it was an active waterway for trade, bringing goods downriver on barges. The canal, which winds around New Hope and some of the nearby towns, gives the area a charm all its own.

I took some pictures in the stone basement of the Black Bass, where the apparition has been seen over the years. Imagine my surprise when there appeared in the picture a white shape which could not be reasonably explained as anything but the boatsman (who, coincidentally, was also named Hans) putting in an appearance for me! He had died in a violent argument with another skipper, and apparently felt that the argument—and his own death—remains unresolved.

How to get there

From New York and other points north and east, you should take the New Jersey Turnpike to I-78 West. From there, find I-287 South to Route 202 South and then over the Delaware River Toll Bridge. Take your first right onto Route 32 South; you will reach Lumberville.

From Philadelphia and other points south and west, take I-95 North to the New Hope Exit (31). Make a left at the stop sign onto Taylorsville Road. Continue approximately 5 miles on Taylorsville Road. At the stop sign, turn left onto Route 32 North (River Road), and follow it for approximately four miles into New Hope, and then another 8 miles north to Lumberville.

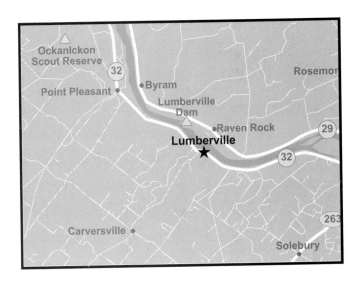

Nearby accommodations

THE BLACK BASS INN
3774 River Road, Lumberville, PA 18933.
(215) 297-5770

INN AT PHILLIPS MILL
2590 N River Road, New Hope, PA 18938
(215) 862-2984 $

1740 HOUSE
3690 River Road, Lumberville, PA 18933
(215) 291-5661 $$$

The Maco Light
Wilmington, North Carolina

There are haunted crossroads, haunted airports—even haunted railroad crossings. One of the most famous of such phenomena is the railroad crossing near Maco, North Carolina, 12 miles west of Wilmington on the Atlantic Coast Line Railroad. Since 1867, an itinerant light has been observed by hundreds of people in the area, and could not be explained on natural grounds.

I interviewed dozens of witnesses; several had not only seen a light approach along the tracks where no light should be, but also, on getting closer, had observed that the light appeared to be inside an old railroad lantern. Some even heard the sound of an approaching train close by. The consensus was that a ghostly personality appears at the Maco trestle holding a railroad lantern aloft as if to warn someone or something. This fits in with the tradition that a man named Joe Baldwin is behind the haunting.

Baldwin was a conductor on what was then the Wilmington, Manchester and Augusta Railroad. He was riding in the end coach of a train one night in 1867, when the coach somehow uncoupled from the train. Baldwin grabbed a lantern in an effort to signal a passenger train following close behind, but unfortunately, the engineer of that train did not see his signal; the trains collided. The only one killed was Joe Baldwin, who was decapitated. His signal lantern was later found a distance from the track. There is no question in my mind that the surviving spirit of Joe Baldwin—who, incidentally, is buried in a cemetery close by the tracks—is still trying to discharge what he considers his duty. Unfortunately, he is not aware of the fact that a train is no longer following him.

Those wishing to watch for the ghostly light at Maco, North Carolina, can do so freely, but must exercise patience, for the ghost does not appear all the time!

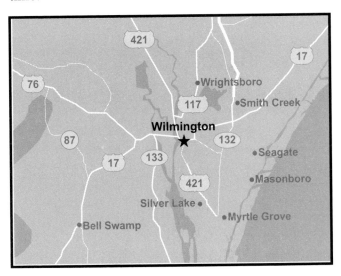

How to get there
The crossing is 12 miles west of Wilmington, North Carolina on the Atlantic Coast Line.

Nearby accommodations

CATHERINE'S INN
410 S Front St.
(910) 251-0863 $

THE WORTH HOUSE
412 S Third St.
(910) 762-8562 $$

GRAYSTONE INN
100 S Third St.
(910) 763-2000 $$$

Knox Lesesne House, College of Charleston

Charleston, South Carolina

Founded in 1770 and chartered in 1785, the College of Charleston is a respected seat of learning and research—sometimes referred to as the Athens of the South. The College itself is the oldest institution of its kind in South Carolina, and the thirteenth oldest institution of higher learning in the United States.

One of the oldest buildings at the College is the Knox Lesesne House—a quaint and historic residence hall in the north central section of campus. Built in the early 19th century, Lesesne is famous today not for its history, but for a tragedy that occurred over one hundred years ago.

During the War Between the States, a young woman committed suicide in the house. At this point in history, Lesesne house was in use as a Confederate barracks, and the young woman was probably romantically involved with one of the soldiers. Beyond that, the details and motivation behind her death are unclear, but she remains a very real part of Knox Lesesne House to this day.

There have been sightings of a young woman in the lobby downstairs and in an upstairs study lounge—she appears always in white. On a visit there a few years ago, I took a photograph of a seemingly empty room, when I developed the film, there was a white female figure in the picture.

How to get there

BARKSDALE HOUSE
27 George St.
(803) 577-4800 $$$

MAISON DU PRE
317 E Bay St.
(803) 723-8691 $$$

HAMPTON INN-HISTORIC DISTRICT
345 Meeting St.
(803) 723-4000 $$

The Ghostly Beachcomber
Pawley's Island, South Carolina

The sandy beaches of South Carolina's low country are both beautiful and lonely. Not far from Georgetown, off the coast, lies sprawling Pawley's Island, named for Percival Pawley, who owned it many years ago.

Known as the oldest resort community in the United States, Pawley's Island was home to some of the most affluent plantation owners in the South—growers of rice and indigo. The narrow strand of land is the home of 600 cottages and houses (no stores, restaurants or hotels) used almost exclusively in the summer months.

Whenever there is approaching danger, such as one of the frequent hurricanes that plague this part of the coast, people report a strange, gray man standing or walking on the dunes. But when they get closer, he dissolves into thin air. The Gray Man supposedly wants to alert people to the approaching storm.

Local businessman William Collins absolutely refused to believe in ghosts, even local ones. During a hurricane watch in 1954, he was walking down the dunes of Pawley's Island to check on the rising surf early in the morning. He thought he was alone, but standing on the beach was a man looking out to sea. Collins assumed it was one of his neighbors, so he called out to the man, but the stranger did not respond.

The weather report assured the islanders that the hurricane had shifted directions and was not likely to hit the area at all. So Collins and his family went to bed that night, no longer worried about the danger. At 5 a.m. Collins was roused from deep sleep by a heavy pounding on his door. When he opened it, he could feel the house shake from a rising wind which had, after all, hit the island.

A stranger stood on his verandah, wearing a fishing cap, common work shirt and pants—all of it gray. The man curtly told Collins to get off the beach, as the storm was heading their way. Collins thanked the stranger and ran upstairs to wake his family. When he came back just a few minutes later, the stranger had disappeared.

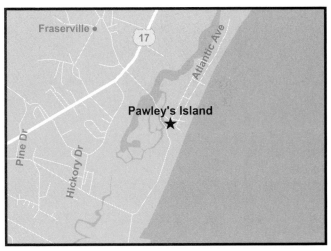

How to get there

Pawley's Island lies off the coast near Litchfield Beach, on Route 17, just 10 miles north of Georgetown and approximately 20 miles south of Myrtle Beach.

Nearby accommodations

CLARION CARRIAGE HOUSE-CAROLINIAN INN
706 Church St, Georgetown, SC 29440
(803) 546-5191 $

1790 HOUSE
630 Highmarket St, Georgetown, SC 29440
(803) 546-4821 $$

SHERATON
2701 S Ocean Blvd, Myrtle Beach, SC 29577
(803) 448-2518 $$$

The Alamo
San Antonio, Texas

The Alamo was originally a small chapel, built by a group of Franciscan monks in 1718. The first building in San Antonio de Valero, as it was called at the time, the little chapel was named Alamo for the cotton-wood grove that surrounded it.

Later, it was expanded into a mission and fortress, meant to as a stronghold for Texas in the conflict with the Mexicans over who had rightful claim to the land. In March, 1836, the president of Mexico General Antonio Lopez de Santa Ana and 4000 troops laid siege to the Alamo, and most of its 188 defenders died in the ensuing 11-day battle. 30 U.S. non-combatants were spared, but the rest of the garrison died at the hands of the larger army. Losses for the Mexicans totaled over 1600 dead and many more wounded. The siege at the Alamo became a landmark event in Texas history, and "Remember the Alamo" was a rallying cry for Sam Houston, Sydney Sherman and their troops in the Battle of San Jacinto, in April of the same year.

But, in January of that year, just prior to the final onslaught, the defenders took their valuables and personal mementos and placed them in one of the mission bells. The bell was buried deep beneath the fort. All sorts of stories are told as to what still lies buried underneath the Alamo, including silver and gold treasure. A private group, Tesoro de Alamo Preservation Society, has been excavating since 1995 and has found some interesting artifacts, but of an earlier period.

There are recurring accounts which describe a ghost on top of the Alamo, walking frantically to and fro as if in search of an escape. Since the reputed treasure has not yet been found, it may well be that the ghost that paces the roof of this historic site is concerned about it still.

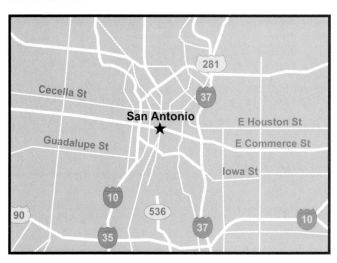

How to get there

The Alamo is smack in the middle of busy San Antonio, Texas, and open to visitors at all times. There are tours (and a lot of crowds) in the daytime, but it is also dramatic place at night, even though you can't get inside. The nearby Riverwalk area has a multitude of great restaurants, shopping, hotels and boat rides that ensure a great visit to San Antonio, whether or not you have your own ghostly encounter.

Nearby accommodations

RADISSON DOWNTOWN MARKET SQUARE
502 W Durango
(219) 224-7155 $

MARRIOTT RIVERCENTER
101 Bowie St.
(210) 223-1000 $$$

YELLOW ROSE
229 Madison
(210) 229-9903 $$$

The Postmaster's House
Charlottesville, Virginia

One of the most charming and also historically important houses in Charlottesville, Virginia, is the home of the local postmaster, a man fully aware of the history all around him, who has taken excellent care of the old house. It is known locally as "the Farm."

On June 14, 1781, American John Jouett spotted Colonel Banastre Tarleton approaching Charlottesville with his battalion of British soldiers, who had been badly defeated in the Battle of the Cowpens in North Carolina earlier in the year. Jouett rode to Charlottesville warn Thomas Jefferson and the legislature of the approaching British, but it was to no avail. When Tarleton finally got to Charlottesville later that day, proceeding along the Old Kings' Highway and destroying several wagonloads of Continental supplies on the way, he thwarted the carefully laid plans of the 200 men to whom the defense of the village had been entrusted. As Tarleton entered Charlottesville, he saw the Farm, and decided to make it his headquarters for the night, and many believe that the ghostly sightings that have occurred in this historic home are connected to Tarleton and his role in the bloody American Revolution.

We can not be sure who exactly the ghosts are, and they may just be psychic impressions from the past. Regardless, there have been a number of encounters in the postmasters house, and it is worth a visit for historical or parapsychological reasons.

How to get there

Historic Charlottesville, Virginia was briefly the nation's capital and has many interesting and important sites. The postmaster's house is in the middle of town and can't be missed. While you are there, visit the University of Virginia, whose Jeffersonian architecture and beautifully manicured campus is truly a treasure of the American South.

Nearby accommodations

HOLIDAY INN
1600 Emmet St.
(804) 293-9111 $

200 SOUTH STREET
200 South St.
(804) 979-0200 $$

OMNI CHARLOTTESVILLE
235 W Main St.
(804) 971-5500 $$$

Castle Hill

Charlottesville, Virginia

The area around Charlottesville, Virginia, abounds with haunted houses—not surprising, since this was once the hub of the young American republic. Its government had its capital, if only briefly, in Charlottesville.

Castle Hill is one of the area's historical landmarks. It is not open to visitors, but it is conceivable that prior arrangements with the owners could be made for a student of history to make a visit.

The house's pink bedroom is the center of ghostly activities. Whenever guests sleep here, they invariably complain of disturbances during the night. Writer Julian Green, a firm skeptic, left the next morning in great hurry. When Amelie Rives, noted novelist, stayed at Castle Hill, she spoke of a strange perfume in the room that was not her own. The ghostly manifestations go back a long time, but no one knows exactly who is attached to the room.

From the testimony of various guests, it appears that the ghost is a woman, not very old, rather pretty, and at times playful. Her intentions seem to be to frighten people using the room. Curiously, however, a few guests have slept in it without hearing uncanny noises or footsteps. Legend has it that those the lady ghost likes may sleep peacefully in "her" bedroom, while those she does not must be frightened away.

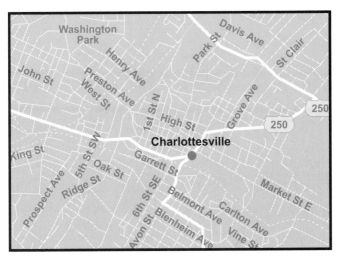

How to get there

Also in Charlottesville, and also subject to permission, but important as an historic landmark, is Castle Hill. It, too, is right in town.

Nearby accommodations

HOLIDAY INN
1600 Emmet St.
(804) 293-9111 $

200 SOUTH STREET
200 South St.
(804) 979-0200 $$

OMNI CHARLOTTESVILLE
235 W Main St.
(804) 971-5500 $$$

The Michie Tavern

Charlottesville, Virginia

Taverns in the eighteenth and early nineteenth centuries were not simply bars or inns; they were meeting places where people could talk freely,about work, love and even politics. They were used as headquarters for Revolutionary movements or for invading military forces. Most taverns of any size had ballrooms in which the social functions of the area could be held. Only a few private individuals were wealthy enough to have their own ballrooms built into their manor houses.

What is fortunate about Michie Tavern is the fact that everything is pretty much as it was in the eighteenth century, and whatever restorations have been undertaken are completely authentic. I visited the allegedly haunted tavern in the company of my psychic friend, Ingrid, for whom this was a first visit to Charlottesville.

Ingrid kept looking into various rooms, sniffing out the psychic presences, as it were, while I followed close behind. We arrived in the third-floor ballroom of the old tavern, and there were impressions of a lively party still lingering in the room. I asked Ingrid what she had felt in the various rooms below. "In the pink room on the second floor I felt an argument or some sort of strife... I'm impressed with an argument over a woman here," Ingrid continued. "It has to do with one of the dignitaries, and it is about one of their wives." Further historical research uncovered that Thomas Jefferson was a regular visitor here, and further psychic investigation has led me to the conclusion that he is indeed involved in the haunting.

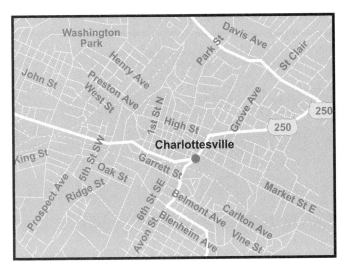

How to get there

The Michie Tavern can be found at 683 Thomas Jefferson Parkway, and reached by phone at (804) 977-1234.

Nearby accommodations

HOLIDAY INN
1600 Emmet St.
(804) 293-9111 $

200 SOUTH STREET
200 South St.
(804) 979-0200 $$

OMNI CHARLOTTESVILLE
235 W Main St.
(804) 971-5500 $$$

Monticello

Charlottesville, Virginia

Monticello was the home of Thomas Jefferson, who designed the entire manor himself and who lies buried here in the family graveyard. It stands on a hill looking down into the valley of Charlottesville, perhaps 15 minutes from the town. Carefully landscaped grounds surround the house

But it was the little honeymoon cottage behind the main house that attracted my psychic friend, Ingrid, more than the main house. Built in the same classical American style as Monticello itself, the two-story cottage has two fair-sized rooms. A walk leads to the entrance to the upper story, but it is not part of the public tour area.

Apparently, Jefferson had a penchant for romantic wanderings. His associations were many and varied, which did not contribute to Mrs. Jefferson's happiness. It seems as if the tension between them has lingered in the little cottage—perhaps Jefferson is unable to reconcile himself with his romantic choices, or perhaps he is clinging to a place where he found much happiness.

There are extensive tours and an excellent Visitors Center not far from the grounds. Monticello is open 8am-5pm March through October, and 9am-4:30pm November through February. Both the house and the Visitors Center are open every day of the year except Christmas. For more information, you should call the Monticello Public Affairs Office at (804) 984-9822.

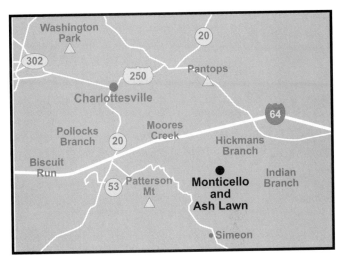

How to get there

Monticello is in the heart of the Virginia Piedmont, about 2 miles southeast of Charlottesville and approximately 125 miles from Washington DC. From I-64, take exit 121 to Route 20 South. To go to the Visitors Center, turn right at the first stoplight; to go to Monticello, turn left on Route 53 just before you reach the stoplight. The entrance is a little over a mile from Route 20 on the left.

Nearby accommodations

HOLIDAY INN
1600 Emmet St.
(804) 293-9111 $

200 SOUTH STREET
200 South St.
(804) 979-0200 $$

OMNI CHARLOTTESVILLE
235 W Main St.
(804) 971-5500 $$$

The Haunted Chair at Ash Lawn

Charlottesville, Virginia

Even furniture can be the recipient of ghostly attention. Not very far from Castle Hill, Virginia, is one of America's important historical buildings: the country home once owned by former president James Monroe, where he and Thomas Jefferson often conversed and may have made major political decisions. This house, small and cozy, was James Monroe's favorite even after he moved to the bigger place that became his stately home later in his career. At Ash Lawn he could get away from affairs of state and public attention to discuss matters of great concern with his friend Jefferson, who lived only two miles away at Monticello.

The ghostly occurrences center around a wooden rocking chair in the main room, which has been seen to rock without benefit of human hands. I don't know how many people have actually seen the chair rock, but Mrs. J. Massey, who lived in the area for many years, said to me when I visited, "I will tell anyone and I have no objection to its being known, that I've seen not once but time and time again the rocking chair rocking exactly as though someone were in it. My brother, John, has seen it too. Whenever we touched it, it would stop rocking."

Monroe's alma mater, the College of William & Mary in Williamsburg, has made and continues to make considerable efforts toward the preservation and restoration of the estate. It is a museum, a site for summer children's festivals, a venue for traditional concerts and opera, and a Christmas tree farm. Call their General Information number, (804) 293-9539, for details on planning a visit.

Admission for adults is $7, Seniors & AAA members get in for $6.50, Children aged 6-11 and local residents pay $3. The estate (unless there is a concert or other planned evening event) is open from 9am to 6pm (March-October) and 10am to 5pm (November-February).

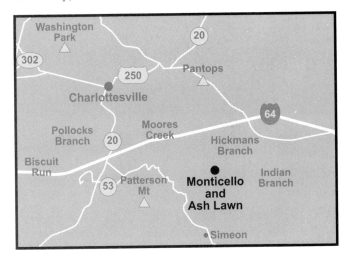

How to get there

The Ash Lawn estate is on the James Monroe Parkway (Highway 795) just southeast of Charlottesville. Exit I-64 at exit 121 to Route 20 south; turn left onto Route 53 just before the stoplight, follow it to 795, and there will be signs directing you to Ash Lawn.

Nearby accommodations

HOLIDAY INN
1600 Emmet St.
(804) 293-9111 $

200 SOUTH STREET
200 South St.
(804) 979-0200 $$

OMNI CHARLOTTESVILLE
235 W Main St.
(804) 971-5500 $$$

Westover

Richmond, Virginia

The magnificent estate of Westover on the James River is foremost among Virginia manor houses. Built in 1730 by William Byrd II, the man who founded Richmond, it stands amid an 11,000-acre working farm, and includes formal gardens. It is not designed to be the home of a country squire, but of a statesman of great wealth.

Colonel Byrd took his daughter, Evelyn, to London for the coronation of King George I in 1717. Evelyn was 18 years old and her father decided to leave her in England to be educated. Soon he received disquieting news from his confidants at the London court that Evelyn had been seen with a certain Charles Mordaunt, and that the two young people were desperately in love. Normally this would be a matter for rejoicing, but not in this case. Charles was an ardent Roman Catholic and grandson of the Earl of Peterborough. Colonel Byrd was politically and personally a staunch Protestant, and the idea of his daughter marrying into the enemy camp, so to speak, was totally unacceptable to him. Immediately he ordered her to return to Westover, and Evelyn had no choice but to obey.

Evelyn quite literally "pined away" to death. Some weeks before her death, however, she had a very emotional discussion with her best friend, Anne Harrison. The two girls were walking up a hill when Evelyn, feeling faint, knew that her days were numbered. She promised her friend that she would return after her death.

The following spring, after Westover had somehow returned to a degree of normalcy after the tragedy, Mrs. Harrison was walking in the garden, sadly remembering what had transpired the year before. Suddenly she saw her old friend standing beside her in a dazzling white gown. Evelyn has appeared from time to time to a number of people, those who live in the area and those who are guests at Westover.

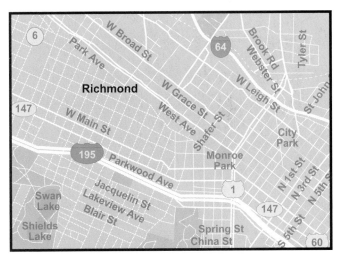

How to get there

Westover is still privately owned, despite its huge fame. Situated two miles above the James River in Richmond, the house itself can be visited only with permission, but the gardens where the phenomena occurred are open to the public.

Nearby accommodations

WILLIAM CATLIN HOUSE
2304 E Broad St.
(804) 780-3746 $$

COURTYARD BY MARRIOTT
6400 W Broad St.
(804) 282-1881 $$

OMNI
100 S 12th St.
(804) 344-7000 $$$

The Woodrow Wilson House

Washington, D.C.

The Woodrow Wilson House, at 2340 S Street in Washington, D.C., is a pleasant residence built in 1915. In 1920, toward the end of his second term in office, President Wilson and his second wife, Edith Bolling Wilson, acquired it as a residence. Wilson died in 1924, Mrs. Wilson in 1961, and the house became, and still is now, under the wing of the National Trust. It is readily accessible and kept up as a museum in the period of Wilson's presidency.

Rumors of psychic phenomena go back almost to the time of Mrs. Wilson's passing, and it was in 1969 that Jose Vasquez, the houseman, witnessed phenomena he could not very well explain.

"Someone" was standing behind him when he played the piano downstairs. In the president's bedroom upstairs, loud footsteps were clearly audible, yet nobody was seen walking. Someone, it seems, was active in the house, and when word got to me about it, I brought Ethel Johnson Meyers with me to Washington. In the seance that followed, while she was in deep trance, President Wilson spoke through her about his struggle for the brotherhood of man, and about looking forward to the year when enemies would join hands for world peace. This he foresaw happening in 1989.

It was in 1989 that the former Soviet Union went out of business, and Russia and America became friends. Remember, Mr. Wilson said this in 1969!

How to get there

The Woodrow Wilson House is open to the public and maintained as a museum. It is located at 2340 S Street in Washington, D.C.

Nearby accommodations

HOWARD JOHNSON KENNEDY CENTER
2601 Virginia Ave. NW
(202) 965-2700 or (800) 654-2000 $

HOLIDAY INN CAPITOL HILL
415 New Jersey Ave. NW
(202) 638-1616 or (800) 638-1116 $

FOUR SEASONS
2800 Pennsylvania Ave. NW
(202) 342-0444 or (800) 332-3442 $$$

The Octagon
Washington, D.C.

Built on the orders of Colonel John Tayloe in 1800 as his town house in the new capital, this mansion stands in one of the most fashionable parts of Washington at the corner of New York Avenue and 18th Street. Originally surrounded by empty land, today it is at the center of several avenues of mansions and expensive town houses.

Even before the house was finished, General Washington spent time there, and during the British occupation of the capital when the White House was burned down, the Octagon served as temporary White House to President Madison and his wife, Dolly. Here Madison signed a peace treaty with Britain in 1815. After the death of Mrs. John Tayloe in 1855, the building passed into other hands and was for a time used as a school for girls.

The Octagon has three stories; downstairs is a magnificent rotunda from which a staircase leads to the upper floors. This staircase is the focus of ghostly activities in the mansion. Most of the reported and witnessed phenomena took place on the second-floor landing, near the banister on the third floor and on the ground floor where a carpet keeps flinging itself back when there is no one about.

Ghostly phenomena had been reported as far back as the mid-19th century and include footsteps, the sound of a plaintive female voice, and other signs of human presences when no one was seen. A long list of observers experienced psychic phenomena here.

The reason for the haunting harks back to the stern Colonel Tayloe. One of his daughters had fallen in love with the wrong kind of man, and Colonel Tayloe would have no part of it. The daughter committed suicide by jumping from the second-floor landing; she fell and broke her neck on the very spot where the carpet keeps flinging itself back. However, the heavy footsteps, clearly belonging to a man, are thought to be those of the distraught father who indirectly caused his daughter's death.

How to get there

The Octagon, at the corner of New York Avenue and 18th Street, in Washington, D.C., is now the head-quarters of the American Institute of Architects, and semi-public. A visit is not difficult.

Nearby accommodations

HOWARD JOHNSON KENNEDY CENTER
2601 Virginia Ave. NW
(202) 965-2700 or (800) 654-2000 $

HOLIDAY INN CAPITOL HILL
415 New Jersey Ave. NW
(202) 638-1616 or (800) 638-1116 $

FOUR SEASONS
2800 Pennsylvania Ave. NW
(202) 342-0444 or (800) 332-3442 $$$

The Ghosts at the White House

Washington, D.C.

This is not about any skeletons that may or may not be hidden in the White House, politically speaking. It is a fact that bona fide ghosts do inhabit the place. There is, first of all, President Lincoln, who has appeared to a number of witnesses, and there is also a report about Dolley Madison putting in an appearance. People who had slept in the Lincoln bedroom reported someone knocking at the door, but when they got up and opened it, there was no one to be seen.

Witnesses include the late Queen Wilhelmina of the Netherlands, Margaret Truman, and various others. I have no idea if more recent guests in that famous bedroom have had any spectral visitors—maybe Abe Lincoln complaining, "Who's been sleeping in MY bed?"

Some of the visions reported about past events in the White House are, however, psychic imprints, not real ghosts.

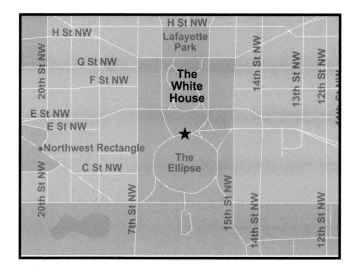

How to get there

The White House ghosts, especially the gentleman who frequents the Lincoln Bedroom, may not be "in" when you take the official tour, which is easy to do (regular tours of the White House include the haunted areas). The address is 1600 Pennsylvania Avenue.

Nearby accommodations

HOWARD JOHNSON KENNEDY CENTER
2601 Virginia Ave. NW
(202) 965-2700 or (800) 654-2000 $

HOLIDAY INN CAPITOL HILL
415 New Jersey Ave. NW
(202) 638-1616 or (800) 638-1116 $

FOUR SEASONS
2800 Pennsylvania Ave. NW
(202) 342-0444 or (800) 332-3442 $$$

INTERNATIONAL
HAUNTED PLACES

The Mackenzie House
Toronto, Ontario

At 82 Bond Street in downtown Toronto was the home of the city's first mayor, William Lyon Mackenzie. The bedroom where he died in 1861 has a strong atmosphere of gloom reported by many visitors.

For a while, the house was an office adjunct to the Canadian Broadcasting Corporation, headquarters for their radio network. Because several caretakers complained about the presence of ghosts, the CBC took the unusual step of calling in a minister, the Canon C.J. Frank, to exorcise the house. Since he could not locate a formal exorcism text, Frank made up an appropriate prayer for the souls of the earthbound spirits in the place. A local specialist on ghost lore, television hostess and reporter Eileen Sonin, revisited the house after the exorcism and found it calmer.

The CBC also formerly owned a building at 90 Sumach Street, where a ghost—a thin man dressed in black—has been seen on the fourth floor near the elevator. Eileen Sonin proved that this specter was connected with a brewery that had been on the same lot before the present building. One of its workers died in an explosion there at the turn of the century, on the fourth floor!

Both buildings can be visited without any difficulty.

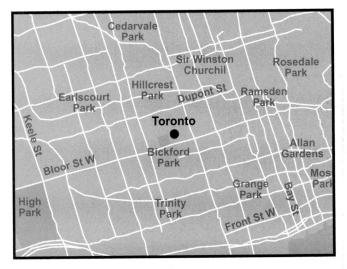

How to get there

Both houses are easily found in the center of Toronto. 82 Bond Street is kept up as a local museum with free access to tourists; 90 Sumach Street is still an open office building easy to visit without questions being asked.

Nearby accommodations

JOURNEY'S END HOTELS
262 Carlingvue Dr. (near Rte 427 & the airport)
(905)624-8200 or (800) 668-4200 $

GUILD INN
201 Guildwood Parkway, Scarborough, Ontario M1E 1P6
(416) 261-3331 $$

PARK PLAZA HOTEL
4 Avenue Rd. at Bloor St. W
(416) 924-5471 or (800) 977-4197 $$$

The Ghost at Toronto University

Toronto, Ontario

A ghost has been observed at the University College in an area known as the Arcade of the Cloisters, part of the old university buildings.

This ghost has been there a long time; students encountered him as long ago as the 1890s. Even before that, a registrar named Falconbridge encountered the apparition in 1866, and described him as a bearded man wearing a conical hat. Another witness,

Beadle McKim, saw the ghost near the main tower and challenged him, whereupon the figure vanished into thin air. When Sir Alan Aylesworth, a well-known Toronto personality, was a student, he met a stranger in the Arcade and invited him for a drink; they had a hot toddy together in his residence. The stranger confided that he was a stone mason named Ivan Reznikoff, who had worked on the building of the College.

The story goes that Reznikoff had gotten into a fight with a fellow mason over a girl, and at the top of the central tower, Ivan was knifed to death and thrown from the tower. After a fire at the university in 1890, some human bones, a skull, and a belt buckle were found at the bottom of the tower well, according to the account researched by Eileen Sonin.

How to get there

Access to Toronto University is in no way restricted, and the visitor might ask to be directed to the area known as the Arcade of Toronto College, where the reported hauntings occurred.

Nearby accommodations

JOURNEY'S END HOTELS
262 Carlingvue Dr. (near Rte 427 & the airport)
(905)624-8200 or (800) 668-4200 $

GUILD INN
201 Guildwood Parkway, Scarborough, Ontario M1E 1P6
(416) 261-3331 $$

Park Plaza Hotel
4 Avenue Rd. at Bloor St. W
(416) 924-5471 or (800) 977-4197 $$$

Rose Hall Greathouse

Montego Bay, Jamaica

Sometimes referred to as the most haunted house in the Western Hemisphere, Rose Hall is the Greathouse of the former Rose Hall Plantation, one of the largest estates of Colonial Jamaica. You will find Rose Hall, now a historic trust property, greatly restored from its former ruined glory, but the original walls (built in the 1770s) still stand.

To this day, some Jamaicans will not go near the house, however, referring to it as filled with "duppies," a local term for ghosts. They are indeed right. The earthbound spirit of Annie Palmer, once mistress of Rose Hall, has never been laid to rest.

Palmer was a sadistic woman who first made lovers of some of her handsomer slaves, then tortured them to death. She was also rumored to have killed three or four husbands. Eventually fate caught up with her, and she was put to death by the last lover she tormented. Much violence and hatred cling to the old masonry.

Palmer, also referred to as "the White Witch of Rose Hall," is buried in a nearby cemetery. The atrocities she committed force her to remain tied to what was once her mansion. I do not doubt she is still there.

The vaulted cellars, where most of the violence occurred, are the principal haunted areas; there is a museum in the basement. For more information, call the Jamaica Tourist Board at (800)233-4582

How to get there
The plantation is not far from the Montego Bay airport, and a good road leads to it. It is not to be confused with a similarly named hotel resort on the same road. From the airport, have your hotel arrange for a JUTA van to drive you; the fare will be metered.

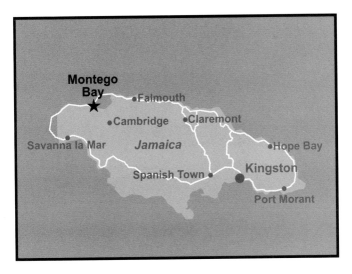

Nearby accommodations
HOLIDAY INN SUNSPREE RESORT
(809) 953-2486 or (800) 352-0731 $$$

SANDALS MONTEGO BAY
(809) 952-5510 or (800) 726-3257 $$$

BONNIE VIEW PLANTATION HOTEL
Port Antonio, (809) 993-2752 $$

The Imperial Palace
Vienna, Austria

This castle was the ancient seat of Austria's emperors, and before that, the Holy Roman Emperors. The building is medieval, but there have been many additions undertaken over the years. The major portion of the "Old Castle" of Vienna was constructed after 1400. The 13th- and 14th-century wing is called "Schweizerhof," or Swiss Court.

Walking up the second floor of this "tract," or portion of the castle, one finds oneself in an area where the walls are two to three yards thick. This section was a small monastery of the Capuchin friars, for the personal use of members of the Imperial family only. Later, this monastery was discontinued and the area became part of the castle. But a ghostly monk has been seen in the area from time to time, walking the dark corridors connecting this ancient portion of the castle with the more modern sections.

A short walk from the monastery area lies a section I have written about, connected with the tragedy of Crown Prince Rudolf and his love Mary Vetsera (the story of these two lovers at Mayerling appears in the following pages). It is an historical fact that Rudolf and Mary met at the Imperial Castle time and again. Mary used a staircase leads from the first to the second floor to gain access to Rudolf's apartment. In the late 1880s, the stairwell nearby was walled up, the door nailed shut, and a heavy closet moved against it to cover any trace of a connecting link between the two floors. Shortly after the tragedy the whitish figure of a woman was observed by witnesses; she comes up the stairs from the lower floor, glides along the corridor, then disappears toward Rudolf's apartment.

How to get there

Everything at the Imperial Palace (The "Hofburg") is open to tourists; the section to look for is the Amalienburg. Look for the stairs leading up, where there is a Marterl or holy shrine in the wall. The Palace is in the very heart of Vienna and cannot be missed.

Nearby accommodations

HAUS TECHNIK
Schäffergasse 2; 01/587-6560-0 $

PENSION CHRISTINA
Hafnersteig 7; 01/533-2961-0 $$

HOTEL-PENSION ZIPSER
Lange Gasse 49; 01/404-54-0 $$$

Mayerling
Lower Austria

Mayerling, which used to be Prince Rudolf of Austria's personal hunting lodge in the 19th century, is now a Carmelite monastery and can be reached by road in about half an hour from Vienna. It can be visited freely, although there is no one to take one behind the principal chapel. This is hardly necessary, since the chapel is at the heart of the tragedy from which the haunting comes.

Before it became a chapel, the building was divided into two floors, the lower being the reception hall of what was then a hunting lodge, and the upper the bedroom in which the Prince Rudolf and his paramour, Mary Vetsera died together. Allegedly the two committed suicide, but other theories abound. One particularly compelling hypothesis is that early on the morning of January 30th, 1889, four men with orders from the Prime Minister of Austria killed the two lovers in their bed. The Emperor Franz Joseph, on hearing the terrible news, ordered the transformation of his son's hunting lodge into a strict Carmelite monastery as a reaction to his son's illicit affair and the resulting tragedy.

There is a considerable amount of photographic evidence that suggests that Prince Rudolf (or perhaps one of his remorseful murderers) still occupies the building. It may be a little tricky to explore the monastery in its entirety, due to the strict nature of the order, but the most haunted areas are still accessible.

How to get there

Mayerling is about a half hour by car from Vienna, or by taxi from nearby Baden, and easy to reach. Take the Autobahn Sued (south) to Baden from Vienna, then follow signs 17 km to Heiligenkreuz (Holy Cross Monastery).

Nearby accommodations

HAUS TECHNIK
Schäffergasse 2; 01/587-6560-0 $

PENSION CHRISTINA
Hafnersteig 7; 01/533-2961-0 $$

HOTEL-PENSION ZIPSER
Lange Gasse 49; 01/404-54-0 $$$

Editor's Note: These hotels are all in Vienna, due to the relatively remote nature of Mayerling.

Schloss Forchtenstein
Austria

Forchtenstein is a yellow compound of imposing
buildings atop a massive hill rising straight out of the
surrounding landscape. This is one of the biggest of
the castles belonging to the Esterhazy family, which
was once one of the most powerful and wealthy families ever to live in Lower Austria and Hungary.

Today, Forchtenstein is run as a museum. Its fortifi-
cations, long, vaulted galleries and rooms, its magnificent collection of paintings and enough medieval and
17th-century arms to equip a small army, make it a
major tourist attraction in this part of Central Europe.
Although it was built in the 14th century, it reached
importance only in the time of the Turkish wars.
During that time, the "Court of Justice" for the entire
land was held here and executions took place in the
courtyard.

When I last visited, my group and I walked past the
monument to Paul Esterhazy, ornamented with bas-
reliefs showing Turkish prisoners of war in chains,
and into the castle itself. Our guide led us up the stairs
onto the roof, which is now overgrown with shrub-
bery and grass.

We followed the guide. The ground was broken

here and showed a small opening, leading back down into the castle.

"What is underneath?" I asked our guide.

"The dungeon," he replied. He didn't believe in ghosts.

I looked down into the dimly lit dungeon. A clammy feeling befell all of us. It was here that the lord of the castle threw his enemies to die of starvation. Once when he was absent from the castle and had left the administration of the household to his wife, Rosalie, she mistreated some of his guests. On his return, he was so angry at her, he had her thrown into this dungeon to die.

Her ghost is said to haunt the castle, although her husband, taken with either remorse or fear of a ghost, built a chapel dedicated to Rosalie on a nearby hill.

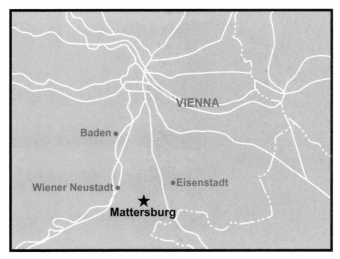

How to get there

Forchtenstein is in Burgenland Province, east of Vienna, near the Hungarian border and about two hours' drive from Vienna. Take Route 16 from Vienna to #50, which will take you to Mattersburg. From there, follow signs to Forchtenstein.

Nearby accommodations

KUR-UND THERMENHOTEL BAD TATZMANNSDORF
Elisabeth-Allee 1, 7431 Bad Tatzmannsdorf
Tel: +43/3353/8940-7160
Fax: +43/3353/8940-7199 $$

SPORTHOTEL RUST
Moerbischer Stasse 1-3, 7071 Rust
Tel: +43/2685/6418
Fax: +43/2685/6478 $$

Schloss Ernegg

Austria

This castle belongs to the Princes Auersberg, and is now operated as a country inn where one can stay a day or a week. The calm surroundings of the countryside and the forest are the prime attractions. The food is simple and good, prices very modest, and the manager speaks excellent English.

The main area of the alleged haunting of the Ernegg is in what is now the owners' apartment. However, even this part of the castle is available to guests during certain parts of the year when the owners are away. Ask the director for the rooms where the ghostly lovers allegedly were seen. The story goes that a young man was courting one of the Auersberg daughters. Since he was only a servant in the castle, Prince Auersberg disapproved. On one such occasion the young man was found in a part of the castle where he had no business. In the manner of the late Middle Ages, he was summarily executed by the castle owner. The ghost of this unfortunate groom is said to haunt that part of the castle now used by the family itself.

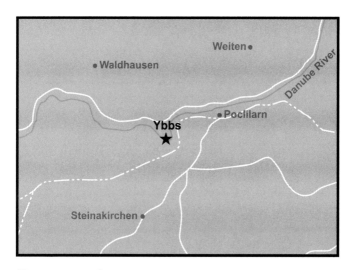

How to get there

Those wishing to visit Ernegg need only address themselves to Mrs. H. Lee, Direcktor, Schloss Ernegg bei Ybbs, Oberösterreich, or Upper Austria, Austria.

Ernegg lies on a country road leading south from the Danube. Ybbs is the nearest large town. Ernegg is about two hours' drive from Vienna, clearly visible from a distance as one approaches. There are also trains and buses to Ybbs, though the easiest way is by car.

Nearby accommodations

HAUS TECHNIK
Schäffergasse 2, Vienna
01/587-6560-0 $

BEST WESTERN SPITZ
Fiedlerstrasse 6, Linz
43 (732) 7364410 $$

AUSTRIA TREND LINZ
Untere Donaulände 9, Linz
43 (732) 76260 $

Editor's note: The first hotel is in Vienna, about
60 miles from Ernegg, the second and third are
in Linz, approximately 30 miles northwest of Ernegg.

Schloss Bernstein

Austria

Bernstein castle was built in the 13th century and has changed hands continuously between Austrian and Hungarian nobles. Since 1892 it has belonged to the Counts Almassy, Hungarian "magnates" or aristocrats.

Count Almassy reports, "I saw by the light of my flashlight a female figure kneeling in front of a wooden Madonna that was placed there in 1914 by my mother when both my brothers and I were away in the war. I had often heard talk of a 'White Lady of Bernstein,' so I realized I was seeing a ghost. She looked like a figure cast in plaster-of-Paris with hard lines. She wore a Hungarian noblewoman's dress of the fifteenth century, with headgear and a big emerald-green stone on her forehead that threw a dim, green light around her. She had her hands folded under her left cheek.

"She is supposed to be an Italian woman, Catherine Frescobaldi. She married Count Ujlocky, of a very old Hungarian family. Her husband was the last King of Bosnia. He was very jealous and he killed her, according to one version, by stabbing her; by walling her in; according to another.

"When I was a boy, I remember every year some-one saw her. When I was in the army, between 1910 and 1913, she was seen many, many times. In 1921 she was seen again when there were Hungarian occupation troops garrisoned at Bernstein during the short-lived Austro-Hungarian campaign of that year—and the ghostly lady chased them away!"

How to get there

After visiting Forchtenstein Castle, you may wish to head to Bernstein before returning to Vienna. Bernstein is now run as a hotel and easily accessible by car from Vienna; it lies on Route 50 some 30 miles west of Castle Forchtenstein, in the Province of Lower Austria.

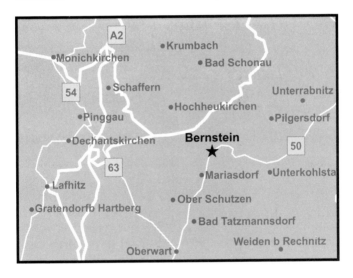

Nearby accommodations

KUR-UND THERMENHOTEL BAD TATZMANNSDORF
Elisabeth-Allee 1, 7431 Bad Tatzmannsdorf
43/3353/8940-7160 $$

STEIGENBERGER BAD TATZMANNSDORF
Am Golfplatz 1, 7431 Bad Tatzmannsdorf
43/3353-8841 $$

Schloss Altenberg

Styria, Austria

Schloss Altenberg is situated near the little village of Hitzendorf, near Graz, capital of the province of Styria, Austria. It can be reached by car in less than a half hour from Graz, and is at present operated as a small guest house where one can stay overnight and have breakfast and dinner. The appointments are very simple and consequently inexpensive; advance reservations are imperative, since Altenberg cannot cope with more than three or four guests at a time.

Some of the reception rooms on the second floor have been turned into guest rooms, and one in particular, looking rather like a chamber for judicial procedures, was the center for our psychic experience. I had the distinct impression of a man in the livery of a bygone age standing in the general vicinity of a large closet and peering at me from sad and rather hollow eyes. The following morning I learned that the closet actually hid a door behind which a corridor led to the outside. As for the man in the old livery, there was a basis in fact.

In the early 19th century, one of the castle owners was on very bad terms with his farmers. When his oppressive tactics aroused them to open rebellion, they searched for him to kill him. His valet helped him hide in the closet area. The rebels could not find him and were thwarted, but the valet later betrayed him to the rebels and saw him killed before his very eyes. His remorseful ghost apparently still finds itself drawn to the scene of his crime.

How to get there

Altenberg is now also run as a modest pension-hotel, and is easily reached by car or taxi from the Styrian capital city of Graz. Graz has a major airport, is a major express train stop, and about 3 hours from Vienna by car or train.

Nearby accommodations

OHNIME
Purbergstrasse 56, Graz
Tel: 43-(316)391143 $

DANIEL
Europaplatz 1, Gra.
Tel: 43-(316)911080 $$

ERZHERZOG JOHANN
Sackstrasse 3-5, Graz
Tel: 43-(316)811616 $$$

The Black Knight of Pflindsberg

Altaussee, Austria

Not far from Altaussee, a picturesque village south-east of Salzburg, stand the remnants of a fortress atop a high ridge. The Romans maintained a guard post there for the north-south trade route pass over which so much of the local salt reached Italy. Access today is from the rear across a deep, man-made moat, although some hardy souls may want to climb up from the front.

According to tradition, during the Middle Ages, one of the last Knights of Pflindsberg had a beautiful daughter who caught the roving eye of a neighbor, the Baron von Wildenstein, Lord of nearby Ischl. She did not care for him, so the gentleman, angry and seeking his conquest at any price, appeared at Pflindsberg with some soldiers and forced the gates.

Meanwhile, the younger brother of the usurper, coincidentally, returned for the first time in many years, to Pflindsberg. Just as he arrived, he found his elder brother, the Baron beating the girl.

Wielding his sword in anger, the younger brother then executed the Baron on the spot. From that moment on, a Knight on a black horse has been reported around Pflindsberg. This legend must have had some basis in fact, for the fortress found no buyer when it and its valuable properties were eventually put up for sale. It was as if a curse adhered to the masonry. Eventually Pflindsberg was abandoned to the elements.

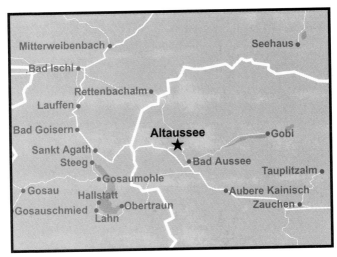

How to get there

Take a train from Vienna or Salzburg to Bad Aussee, or drive south from Salzburg. The fortress is on a rocky outcrop and is easily seen from the road.

Nearby accommodations

SEEVILLA
Fischerndorf 60, 8992 Altausee
43/3622-71302 $$

The Tower

London, England

Probably the most celebrated British royal ghost is the shade of unlucky Queen Anne Boleyn, second wife of Henry VIII, who ended her days on the scaffold. Accused of infidelity, a form of treason in the 16th century, she was decapitated despite protestations of her innocence. Historians have established that she was speaking the truth, but at the time of her trial, it was politically expedient to remove her from the scene, and even her uncle, the trial judge, had no inclination to save her neck.

Anne Boleyn's ghost has been reported in many places connected with her. She has appeared at Hampton Court, as attested by witnesses over the years, and at Windsor Castle, where she is reported to have walked along the eastern parapet. At the so-called Salt Tower within the confines of the Tower of London, a guard observed her ghost walking along headless, and he promptly fainted. That case is on record; the man insisted over and over again that he had not been drinking.

Considering how many people were put to death at the Tower, many if not most for political reasons, more ghosts ought to be reported there, but not even the two young princes murdered on order of Richard III have shown up as ghosts. Some of the psychic imprints of past events do linger on, however, and a sensitive person will experience them. But unlucky Anne Boleyn does seem to be more substantial.

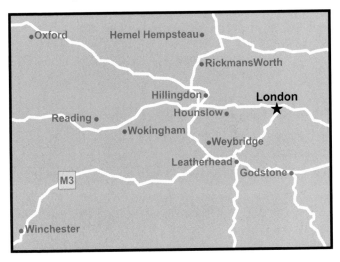

How to get there
Right by the Thames, the Tower is an open tourist attraction of major proportions, and is easily reached by the London Underground trains to Tower Bridge.

Nearby accommodations
NOVOTEL WATERLOO
133-127 Lambeth Road
0171/793-1010 or (800) 221-4542 $

EGERTON HOUSE
17-19 Egerton Terrace
0171/589-2412 or (800) 473-9492 $$

HYDE PARK HOTEL
66 Knightsbridge
0171/235-2000 or (800) 526-6566 $$$

The Ghost at the Hotel Piccadilly

London, England

Ghosts often appear in country inns and remote places, but to find a haunted room in a busy urban hotel is somewhat more unusual. The Hotel Piccadilly is right in the heart of the Piccadilly district of London, and is one of the older, more stately hotels in the British Capital.

A traveler named Evelyn Haley was assigned room #537 some years ago, when she was visiting London with a tour group. Upon entering the room, a powerful chill ran through her body, and she remarked on how unusually the cold the room was. She went into the bathroom to unpack some of her things and felt a strong presence next to her, watching her. She turned around, only to find that the door was closing slowly—all by itself.

Ms. Haley explained to the tour leader that she

could not possible sleep in that room. He agreed and she was moved into another room nearby. Meanwhile, she asked a psychic friend to take a look at the first room; but she shared none of the details of her experience there. He immediately declared, upon entering the room, that someone had committed suicide there, by slitting his wrists in the bathroom.

That night, she returned to her new room, hoping that she would not be troubled by the ghost. But in the middle of the night, her closet door suddenly opened by itself and slammed against the wall with a bang. After she got up and closed the door, it happened again. The door continued to open and slam shut on its own until she finally yelled out to the ghost, imploring it to stop—and stop it did.

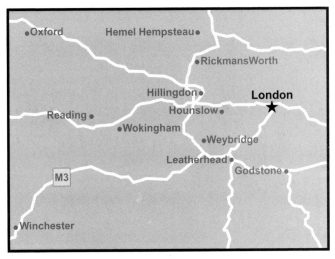

How to get there

The Hotel Piccadilly is on Denman and Piccadilly Streets; the main entrance is on Denman. You may reach the hotel itself at 071-867-1118.

Nearby accommodations

NOVOTEL WATERLOO
133-127 Lambeth Road
0171/793-1010 or (800) 221-4542 $

EGERTON HOUSE
17-19 Egerton Terrace
0171/589-2412 or (800) 473-9492 $$

HYDE PARK HOTEL
66 Knightsbridge
0171/235-2000 or (800)526-6566 $$$

The Grenadier Club

London, England

Tucked away in a quiet mews by Hyde Park stands an old inn called The Grenadier. The Grenadier, with its original pewter bar, is said to be the oldest inn of its kind in London. Originally it was the officers' mess of the Duke of Wellington, located directly outside the barracks. During the reign of King George IV, the inn was known as The Guardsman, and was already famed for its good food and drink. According to The Old Inns of England, "The pub is haunted during September by the ghost of an officer who died due to flogging after being caught cheating at cards."

At the time of my first visit, I had the strange feeling that someone was looking over my shoulder while I was reading the menu. I attributed the feeling to the fact that the inn was very crowded at the time and people were continually walking back and forth between the bar and the dining room to the rear. But on at least one occasion, when I turned around to see who it was, there was absolutely no one nearby. Two Americans who visited the place and took photographs came up with some remarkable psychic photographs, so the place is still "active" in some way.

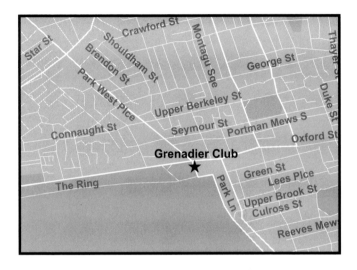

How to get there
The Grenadier is on Old Barrack Yard, on the west side of Hyde Park, and accessible to guests most of the time.

Nearby accommodations
NOVOTEL WATERLOO
133-127 Lambeth Road
0171/793-1010 or (800) 221-4542 $

EGERTON HOUSE
17-19 Egerton Terrace
0171/589-2412 or (800) 473-9492 $$

HYDE PARK HOTEL
66 Knightsbridge
0171/235-2000 or (800) 526-6566 $$$

The Nell Gwyn Town House

London, England

At 69 Deane Street, in the heart of Soho, the London nightclub belt, is a very old house originally built in the 17th century as the Royal Saddlery. Next door used to be the Royalty Theatre, and 69 Deane Street has housed a succession of clubs, mainly strip clubs. Today it is a bar.

King Charles II gave the place to the one woman he truly loved, actress Nell Gwyn, so she would be closer to him in London. She also had a country house in St. Albans.

Unfortunately the king was not always able to be with her, so other men caught her attention. Captain John Molineux of the King's Guards became her lover, the king found out, and a duel to the death was fought between the captain and the men the king had sent to kill him.

Psychic phenomena ranging from footsteps to doors opening by themselves, especially the door to the roof where the fatal duel was fought, had for years frightened the people who worked at the club. I held two seances there with two different mediums, and Nell herself told us what had happened, which proved to be the truth.

Nell may well be bound to the place where her lover died, for it is true that she loved the king, but not with the same passion he had for her.

How to get there

The Nell Gwyn "theatre" is at 69 Deane Street in the heart of Soho, the Greenwich Village of London. The psychic phenomena occurred mainly in the dressing rooms and on the roof.

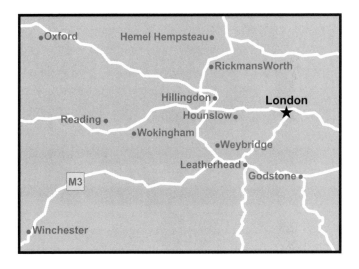

Nearby accommodations

NOVOTEL WATERLOO
133-127 Lambeth Road
0171/793-1010 or (800) 221-4542 $

EGERTON HOUSE
17-19 Egerton Terrace
0171/589-2412 or (800) 473-9492 $$

HYDE PARK HOTEL
66 Knightsbridge
0171/235-2000 or (800) 526-6566 $$$

The Ghostly Roman Soldiers

**Malvern Hills,
Hereford & Worcester, England**

The "British Camp", near Ledbury is actually an artificial hill, an earthenworks, erected by the Romans almost 2000 years ago as a defense position. It is locally known as the Hereford Beacon, and is one of the higher hills in the area. The summit is terraced, and the site is easily accessed.

Mrs. Catherine Warren-Browne, a highly psychic woman who left her native England only recently, had an extraordinary experience in this place when she was a small girl.

When she was just seven years old, she and her family were visiting with an aunt at Little Malvern in Worcestershire. The British Camp is only a mile or so from Little Malvern, and one afternoon little

Catherine and her French governess went for a stroll on the hill. As they were watching some sheep grazing nearby, Catherine heard the heavy tramping of foot soldiers. She wheeled around, only to see a line of Roman soldiers marching steadily over the crest of the hill. They were mainly foot soldiers, but there were also some cavalry on horseback, a standard bearer and literally hundreds in their group. She noticed all the unusual details of their uniforms and arms and pointed them out to her governess, who didn't see anything or anyone. When the column reached the top of the hill, it simply vanished.

The British Camp is about a mile from the center of Little Malvern.

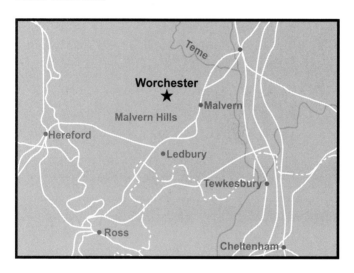

How to get there

Northwest of London on the A35, and just southwest of Birmingham,Malvern Hills is just southwest of Worcester. Keep an eye out for a sign that reads "British Camp"

Nearby accommodations

THE COTFORD HOTEL
51 Graham Road, Malvern
Tel: 01684572427 $

THE COTTAGE IN THE WOOD HOTEL
Hollywell Road, Malvern Wells, Malvern
Tel: 01684575859 $$

SIDNEY HOUSE HOTEL
40 Worcester Road, Malvern
Tel: 01684574994 $$$

Salisbury Hall

Hertfordshire, England

About an hour from London, near St. Albans, Hertfordshire, stands a moderate-size manor house (which used to be the country home of Nell Gwyn, King Charles II's lover) called Salisbury Hall. The area was settled at a very early period in British history, within a few miles of where the Roman city of Verulamium stood. Roman artifacts are frequently dug out of the soil around Salisbury Hall.

The area near the Hall's staircase is where witnesses have seen the ghost of Nell Gwyn. It may strike some readers as curious that a ghost can appear in more than one location, but Nell Gwyn apparently was partially free and allowed herself to be drawn to two places connected with her emotional life.

In addition to Nell, the ghost of a cavalier haunts the upstairs part of the hall. At one time there was an additional wing to the building, which no longer exists; the cavalier has been observed in the corridor leading to

148

that nonexistent wing. In a room at the end of the corridor, the cavalier is said to have committed suicide when pursued by soldiers of Oliver Cromwell. He apparently carried some valuable documents and did not want to have them fall into their hands; nor did he want to be tortured into telling them anything of value. This was at the height of the Civil War in England, when the Cavaliers—partisans of the Royalists—were hotly pursued by the Parliamentary soldiers, also known as the Roundheads. Although the suicide took place in the 1640s, the footsteps of the ghostly cavalier can still be heard on occasion at Salisbury Hall.

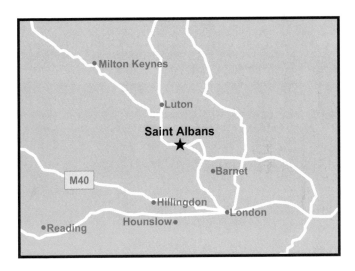

How to get there

Nell's home at the village of St. Albans, Salisbury Hall, can be reached by car or bus from London in about an hour. Take the M1 from London then the A41 directly to St. Albans.

Nearby accommodations

NOVOTEL WATERLOO
133-127 Lambeth Road
0171/793-1010 or (800) 221-4542 $

EGERTON HOUSE
17-19 Egerton Terrace
0171/589-2412 or (800) 473-9492 $$

HYDE PARK HOTEL
66 Knightsbridge
0171/235-2000 or (800)526-6566 $$$

Editor's note: All of the above hotels
are in London.

Hampton Court Palace

Greater London, England

This sprawling residence of kings and queens has several ghosts in it, but the most important ones are Jane Seymour and Catherine Howard.

There is a great deal of difference between these two queens of Henry VIII. Witnesses have seen Jane Seymour coming from what was her apartment in the palace, carrying a lighted taper and walking toward the Silver Stick Gallery.

But matters are very different with Catherine Howard, who did not die a natural death as Jane Seymour did. Catherine (very young) married Henry VIII (very old). She had a lover, and was discovered. The enraged king had her apprehended to be executed immediately; at the time Catherine was in residence at Hampton Court.

As the executioner's men came after her, she took flight along the long corridors shrieking in terror, knowing full well what was coming. Her shrieks have been heard by visitors.

There are also ghosts of lesser stature, such as two skeletons discovered inside the palace in a shallow grave. Nobody knows who they were.

Finally, Mistress Penn, foster-mother to sickly Edward

VI, seems to have returned to her old flat after her grave by the old church in the village was disturbed.

Today, Hampton Court Palace is maintained as an extraordinary "living tapestry of history"—costumed guides and audio tours provide insight into the history of the royal family, the palace and the gardens. The Palace is open year-round, with the exception of December 24-26; admission fees are 8 pounds for adults, 5.75 pounds for Seniors/Students, 4.90 pounds for children under 16, and free for children under 5.

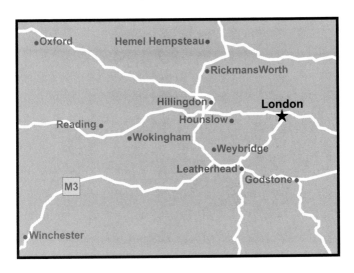

How to get there

Hampton Court lies on the Thames River south of London on A308, close to both the A3 and the M3. It can also be reached easily by train (get off at Hampton Court Station), Underground (to Wimbledon and then go by train), or River Launch from Westminster, Richmond or Kingston.

Nearby accommodations

NOVOTEL WATERLOO
133-127 Lambeth Road
0171/793-1010 or (800) 221-4542 $

EGERTON HOUSE
17-19 Egerton Terrace
0171/589-2412 or (800) 473-9492 $$

HYDE PARK HOTEL
66 Knightsbridge
0171/235-2000 or (800) 526-6566 $$$

The Ghost Monks of Winchester Cathedral

Hampshire, England

Winchester Cathedral is major landmark of England's history—it has been a center of prayer, study history for over 900 years. You can visit the tombs of Jane Austen and Isaac Walton, see the famous and extraordinarily illuminated Winchester Bible and explore the unique collection of Chantry Chapels.

I decided to visit the famed old cathedral at Winchester because of persistent reports of ghostly processions of monks in the church where no monks have trod since the 16th century. If one stood at a certain spot in the nave of the huge cathedral, one might see the transparent monks pass.

Amateur photographer T. L. Taylor thought he was photographing empty choir stalls inside Winchester Cathedral, but the pictures came out with people sitting in the stalls.Taylor took two pictures inside the cathedral; the first shows the choir stalls empty. The second, taken an instant later, shows 13 figures in the stalls, most in medieval costume. Taylor swears he saw no one there.

My own camera is a 15-year-old camera which has a device making double exposures impossible. I use Agfa 120 film, and no artificial light except what I find in the places I photograph. I don't use a flash or floodlights, and have my films developed by commercial labs.

When my film came back from the lab the following day, I checked it carefully. One photo quite clearly showed a transparent procession of hooded monks, seen from the rear, walking on what appeared to be a floor just below present level of the church floor (as a result, they were only visible from the knees up). I did some research on the history of that particular area of the building and found that the floor used to be lower than its present level, so the ghostly monks were walking on the floor level they knew, not ours.

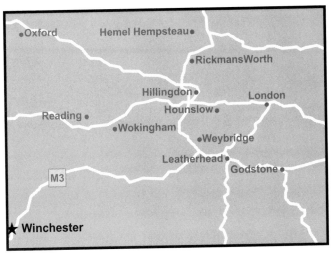

How to get there

Winchester lies in the center of Hampshire, south west of London and just north east of Southampton. From London, take the A30 to the A33, which runs directly into Winchester. The magnificent cathedral and adjoining Visitors' Centre is open to visitors daily. The phenomena of the monks walking usually occurred on rainy days and at 11:00 a.m.

Nearby accommodations

THE WINCHESTER MOATHOUSE
Worthy Lane, Winchester
Tel: (01962) 709-988 $

HARESTOCK LODGE HOTEL & RESTAURANT
Harestock Road, Winchester
Tel: (01962) 881-870 $$

THE BELL HOTEL
West Street, New Alresford, Nr Winchester
Tel: (01962) 732-429 $$

Sawston Hall

Cambridge, England

Sawston Hall lies a short distance from the great English university town of Cambridge. It was once a Catholic stronghold that was an integral part of the conflicts between Catholics and Protestants in England, and has been in the Huddleston family for many generations. Currently, the hall is a highly reputable language school—in the past it has served as a World War II airbase headquarters and has been the set for a number of films and documentaries.

The principal personality associated with Sawston Hall is Queen Mary Tudor, sometimes called Bloody Mary. To escape the wrath of the Protestants after she, a Catholic, was chosen queen, Mary hid overnight at Sawston Hall, and successfully escaped in a disguise the following morning. The Duke of Northumberland, who was so angered that Mary Tudor would have the crown instead of his daughter-in-law Lady Jane Grey, was pursuing Mary Tudor as she made her way to London. Infuriated that she escaped his grasp at Sawston Hall, he burned it down in revenge. Mary

Tudor was so grateful to the Huddlestons for aiding her flight, that she had Sawston Hall completely rebuilt.

People who have slept in the four-poster bed (which survived the fire) where Queen Mary slept that fateful night, have reported uncanny experiences. It is always the same story: three knocks at the door, then the door opens by itself and a gray form slowly floats across the room and disappears into the tapestry. Many have heard the virginal (a predecessor of the organ) play soft music when there was no one in the drawing room. It is a fact that the young Princess Mary was expert at this instrument.

Sawston Hall is architecturally and historically an intriguing and impressive place and the haunting here is an integral part of England's history.

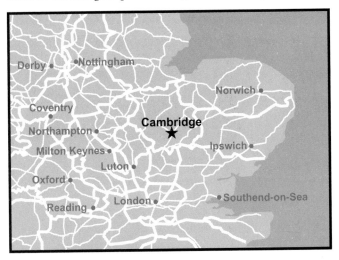

How to get there

Sawston Hall is reached from London on the M11 to Cambridge, where you will see clearly marked signs. The trip will take a few hours, but is worth the time. You can reach the general information number of the language school for more specific directions at: (01223) 835099 within Britain; +44 1223 835099 from overseas.

Nearby accommodations

FORTE POSTHOUSE CAMBRIDGE
(01223) 237-000 $$

REGENT HOTEL
(01223) 351-470 $$$

Longleat Palace

Warminster, Wiltshire/Wessex, England

In the west of England, not far from the city of Bath, stands the huge country house Longleat, seat of the seventh Marquess of Bath, Alexander Thynn. The grandiose Elizabethan house was built in 1540 by Sir John Thynne (the current Lord Bath changed the family name to 'Thynn'), and has been continually added to and expanded by successive generations. In 1949, to help meet the crippling cost of maintaining a manor of such an elaborate estate, the sixth Marquess became the first landowner in Britain to open his estate to the public. Since then, it has evolved into a museum, a drive-in animal park (complete with elephants, rhinos, tigers, giraffes and more), the World's Longest Hedge Maze, an Adventure Castle, Victorian Kitchen and a site for a variety of special events. Especially interesting are the erotic murals painted by the current Lord Bath.

Three sets of ghosts are at Longleat. In the so-called "red library," the apparition of a scholarly-looking man wearing a high collar and the costume of the 16th century has been seen. He is believed to be the builder of Longleat, Sir John Thynne. He may be roaming the corridors for personal reasons connected with the acquisition of the property.

Upstairs is a haunted corridor; its long, narrow passage parallels the bedrooms. The ghost of Louisa

Carteret, one of the ladies of the Bath family, has been repeatedly observed here. She has every reason to be there: On one occasion she was discovered with a lover by the second Viscount Weymouth, one of Lord Bath's ancestors. The viscount fought a duel, and the intruder was killed.

According to British medium Trixie Allingham, the restless ghost of Sir Thomas Thynne, another of Lord Bath's ancestors has been observed in the reception rooms downstairs. Sir Thomas was betrayed by his wife, whose lover had hired two professional assassins to murder her husband. The event took place on the highroad: the murderers stopped a coach bringing Sir Thomas home, dragged him out and killed him. He was drawn back to where his emotions were—his home—and apparently cannot find peace because of the betrayal and murder.

Open daily (except for Christmas Day), Longleat House can be reached for more information at (01985)844-400.

How to get there
Longleat is outside Bath, in Wiltshire, between Warminster and Frome.

Nearby accommodations
THE OLD BELL HOTEL
42 Market Place, Warminster, Tel: (01985) 216-611

THE TALBOT INN
High Street, Mells, Frome, Tel: (01373) 812-254

FARMERS HOTEL
1 Silver Street, Warminster, Tel: (01985) 213-815

The Garrick's Head Inn

Bath, England

Bath is a Regency gem, and the old Garrick's Head Inn is still a major tourist attraction. Psychic disturbances have been well attested to by so-called skeptical reporters, and the inn's manager saw the heavy cash register take off of its own volition one day and fly across the bar. People have also been heard walking where no one was about, especially upstairs where the gambling used to get pretty heady in the old days. Witnesses also described feeling "a kind of cobweb" they had walked into; that's what it feels like when you "walk into" a ghost.

This ghost is a young girl for whose affections two

men were gambling when Beau Nash, infamous gambling lord of the 18th century, owned the place. The rivalry got out of hand and one of the two players was killed, the winner rushing upstairs to claim his "prize." The girl however was not willing—she barricaded herself in the room, and when the winner was about to break down her door, she hanged herself.

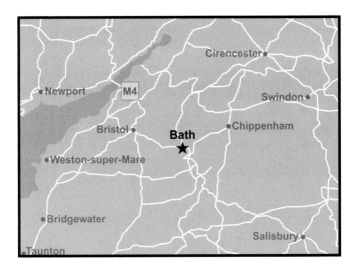

How to get there

In the city of Bath, the Garrick's Head Inn is right next to the Royalty Theatre, and across from the Hotel St. Francis. From London, take the M4.

Nearby accommodations

THE FRANCIS HOTEL
Queen Square
(01225) 424-257 $$

GEORGES HOTEL
2-3 South Parade.
(01225) 464-923 $

BROMPTON HOUSE HOTEL
St. Johns Road
(01225) 420-972 $

The Ghost Monks at Beaulieu

Hampshire, England

The town of Beaulieu, in southern England, is most famous for its National Motor Museum, which contains an historic and world renowned collection of cars and motor bikes. The museum stands on the grounds of the Beaulieu Estate, which is also the home of a Palace House and a 13th Century Abbey. The Abbey is the center of the haunting at Beaulieu.

Ghostly monks have been observed by visitors in the abbey and along the pathways leading toward it. In the chapel, two recent visitors saw the room that was once the monks' dining hall filled with monks eating and going through the routines of mealtime, even though the refectory itself has been used for a different purpose for many years. Others have heard the choir sing in the empty church. Psychic impressions also include the sounds of chanting monks, bells, and other auditory elements from the past. Monks reading scrolls on the stones, walking in what was once a garden, digging a grave in the dead of night to bury one of their own—these are some of the reports of the past decade. Yet the monks' own burial ground has never been discovered; there is a cemetery for the villagers, but no monks are buried there. Could it be that the restless monks are looking for their own burial ground?

Beaulieu is a very small village, with a few select shops and restaurants, and a very charming spot to visit. The Hampshire tourist board has made considerable efforts to welcome and encourage tourism in this area, and the effects are significant: a variety of well-publicized tourist attractions, hotels, restaurants and shops. The village is situated on the Beaulieu River; further down the river is Bucklards Hard, famous for its traditional ship building dating back to the 18th Century.

How to get there

Beaulieu is in the southern-most section of England, just across the Solent Spithead from the Isle of Wight. Southampton is the nearest large town to the north and Bournemouth is just west along the coast.

Nearby accommodations

THE MONTAGU ARMS HOTEL
Palace Lane, Beaulieu
(01590) 612-324 $$$

THE WHITE ROSE HOTEL
Village Centre, Sway, Lymington
(01590) 682-754 $$

STANWELL HOUSE HOTEL
15 High Street, Lymington
(01590) 677123 $$

Camelot
Cadbury, England

During Roman times this was a defensive hill fort. When the Romans turned the area over to an army general named Ambrosius, it became a military strong point for the emerging Britain. Ambrosius' successor as ruler of the local kingdom was Arturius, a career officer. Through centuries of story telling, he eventually became the legendary King Arthur. But the real Arthur and the real Camelot were here, in the early 6th century, not the Middle Ages. Arthur died peacefully in 516 A.D.

When I visited the place in the company of medium Sybil Leek, we were not expecting any ghosts. But to my surprise, when Sybil lapsed into a deep trance, a personality residing in the hill fort manifested, and we had a long conversation about his time. He referred to himself as a bird—a Merle—he was clearly trying to convey that he was a Merlin, or a sorcerer/advisor to the king. "Merlin" was not really a name but an office, a title, and there must have been a number of such Merlins.

Again, legend has taken over reality and created a single character, who embodies and embellishes upon the Merlins. Before you go, check out the legend of the Sword in the Stone and the stories of King Arthur and Camelot for more legend and lore about this area.

If you visit this historic spot, perhaps Merlin will talk to you, too.

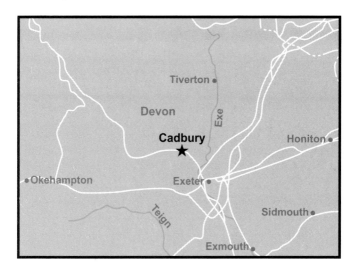

How to get there

Cadbury Hill in South Cadbury, west of Ilchester in Somerset, is easily reached from London by car on the A303. Go to Ilchester, south of London; Camelot is west of the town. Markers are all over the place to direct you.

Nearby accommodations

THE WHITE LION
High Street, Bourton
Tel: 01747840866 $$

THE CATASH INN
North Cadbury
Tel: 01963440248 $$

HOLBROOK HOUSE HOTEL
Holbrook, Wincanton
Tel: 0196332377 $$

Bisham Abbey
Buckingham, England

Giving the impression of a palace rather than a religious residence, the gray-walled abbey has large reception rooms, a magnificent hall, and innumerable bedrooms. One room—occupied at the time of my visit by the establishment's bursar, Cecily de Havas—has been the center of ghostly activity for a long time.

On the Thames River, not far from Marlow, stands

one of the finest Tudor buildings in England: Bisham Abbey. A priory in the 15th century, it became a private house in the 16th century and was passed into the family of Sir Thomas Hoby. Since, it has become a recreation center and a government building: one can visit without prior appointment.

Sir Thomas's wife, Elizabeth, had gone to London on one occasion, forgetting completely that she had sent their child to his room in punishment. She was gone several days, and when she returned the child had died. To her last days she reproached herself for the death of her child. Since her death, her figure has been observed coming from behind the wall in the aforementioned room, with a basin floating ahead of her in which she keeps washing her hands, apparently trying to cleanse them from the blood of her child.

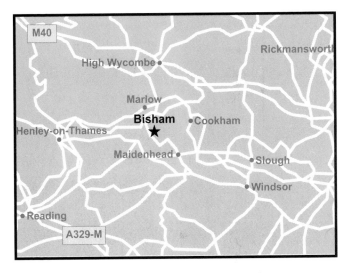

How to get there

Up the Thames from London, near Marlow, Bisham Abbey can be visited without difficulty. It can easily be reached by car or train in somewhat more than an hour. Be sure to seek out the famous haunted wall, from which the ghost of Elizabeth Hoby emerges.

Nearby accommodations

DANESFIELD HOUSE
NR Henley-on-Thames, Marlow
Tel: 44 (1628) 891010 $$$

Blanchland Abbey

Newcastle, England

The Abbey of Blanchland was founded by Pre-
monstratensian monks, a sect that was a strict off-
shoot of the Benedictines. The land on which the
abbey sits was originally part of the old earldom of
Northumbria, appropriated by Henry I for the Norman
de Bolbec family. The family itself added some of their
own lands in 1214, and it was then that the name
Blanchland, which means white land, was mentioned
for the first time. The name is probably derived from
the white habits of the monks. The monastery was
dissolved under Henry VIII, as were all others, and in
1539 the remaining monks were pensioned off, leaving Blanchland Abbey empty after a 400 years tenure.

A group of buildings, including the kitchen and the
prior's house, eventually became an unusual hotel,
the Lord Crewe Arms, owned and operated by the
Vaux Breweries of Sunderland. The stone-vaulted
chamber of the house now serves as a bar.

According to the manager, several villagers have seen the apparition of a woman in the churchyard and in the church next door to the hotel. She was seen walking along the Hexham Road, and opens and shuts doors in the haunted wing of the hotel. People who had slept in the room we were in had at various times complained of a "presence."

How to get there

Blanchland is run as a hotel now, and is easily reached by taxi from the Newcastle-upon-Tyne airport.

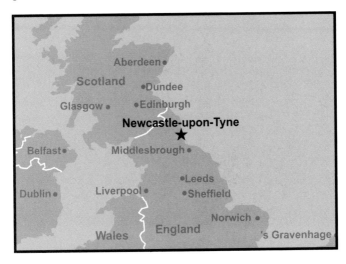

Nearby accommodations

HOSPITALITY INN
Osborne Road
Tel: 44 (191) 2817881 $$

FORTE CREST
New Bridge Street
Tel: 44 (191) 2326191 $$

HOLIDAY INN NEWCASTLE
Great North Road
Tel: 44 (191) 2019988 $$

The Haunted Room
at the Hotel de l'Europe
Avignon, France

The Hotel de l'Europe in Avignon is a distinguished, fashionable hotel famous not only with the French but also wealthy British and American tourists. If you are traveling south from Paris to Nice it is a good place to break the journey.

Room No. 2 is a large, comfortable room on the second floor, furnished with exquisite antiques, yet offering the best in contemporary amenities as well.

In 1945, Capt. George Wood, on the staff of the Duke of Windsor, and his wife, Rose, were occupying this room. Mrs. Wood was awakened in the middle of the night by the feeling that someone was in the room. Fully awake, she saw a man standing in the middle of the chamber. As she challenged the apparition, the man bolted out of the room—straight through the door! The next morning she queried the hotel staff. The apparition was well-known to them.

He was called "The General," though no one knew who he had been.

In 1952, Ruth Thornhill stayed at the Hotel de L'Europe, in room No. 2. She was rudely awakened in the middle of the night. The doors of the wardrobe burst open with great force, and out came a man dressed in the military garb of the 16th century!

He approached her bed, and for an agonizing moment she could actually feel his icy fingers on her hand. Then the specter turned around abruptly and went into the bathroom. Minutes later, when nothing further occurred, Ruth got up and looked in the bathroom. It was empty. As there was no window and no entry other than through the bedroom, no one could have left by natural means.

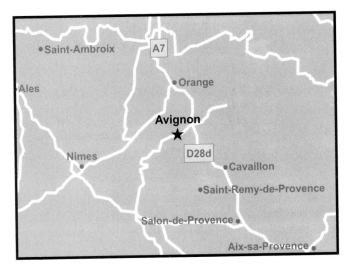

How to get there

The TGV train from Paris to Avignon takes several hours; driving would take all day. You can also fly from Paris.

Nearby accommodations

HOTEL DE L'EUROPE
12 Place Crillon
Tel: 334-9014-7676 $$$

HOTEL AVIGNON PLAZA
26 Place de l'Horloge
Tel: 334-9082-2145 $

BRISTOL HOTEL
44 Cours Jean-Juares
Tel: 334-9082-2121 $$

The Eight Young Ladies of the Château de la Caze

Gorges du Tarn, France

The Château de la Caze is a solid, well-preserved Renaissance castle perched on a hill in the center of the picturesque Gorges du Tarn, in southeastern France. It is not easy to reach because the winding road requires skillful driving. But the country around Caze is of such unusual beauty that it pays for the traveler to take the extra time and descend into the ravine of the Tarn River.

Caze was long eclipsed by the importance of the nearby monastery of St. Enimie. The Abbot's brother had a marriageable daughter named Soubeyrane, engaged to another local dignitary named William Alamand de Montclair. As part of the wedding contract, William and his bride, Soubeyrane, built the strong castle in 1489. Unfortunately, the marriage never happened, so the castle passed into the hands of another family, the Mostuéjouls. The head of the family then was Captain Bertrand de Mostuéjouls, king's lieutenant in the district of Gevaudan, and a famous warrior who had successfully battled the Huguenots. His daughter inherited the castle, and through her marriage to a member of the de Malian family, produced eight lovely daughters. Their portraits still adorn the walls of the castle. Because of their presence, Caze soon became the rallying point for the young men of the district who came to pay court to the eight mademoiselles.

But allegedly the young women could not find proper husbands. Their frustrated ghosts are said to haunt the corridors of the south tower, where their well-guarded quarters had been. Travelers report being disturbed at night by the transparent apparition of one or more young females entering the bedroom as if in search of something or someone.

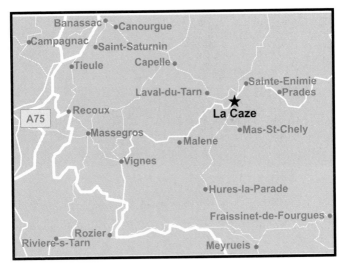

How to get there

La Caze lies in the rough ravine called the Gorges du Tarn (valley of the Tarn River), in Southeastern France, and is best reached by car. The Château de la Caze is now an elegant inn and can be visited without difficulty. The nearest train station is 5 km from La Caze by D907 ("Gorges du Tarn Road") at La Malène, on the Paris-Biziers line. Paris is 620 km away from La Caze, and Biziers is 170 km away.

Nearby accommodations

HÔTEL CHÂTEAU DE LA CAZE
Gorges du Tarn à la Màlene, 48210 Sainte-Enimie
Tel: 33 (0) 4-66-48-51-01 $$$

DU COMMERCE
Gorges du Tarn, Le Pont, 48210 Sainte-Enimie
Tel: 33 (0) 4-66-48-50-01 $

The Old Palace

Berlin, Germany

The Old Palace, or Das Alte Schloss, was the town residence of the kings of Prussia and later of the German Kaiser. It also had a prison area known as the "tower of the green hat", where many died terrible deaths.

Built on the splendid Unter den Linden street, after 1919 the palace was turned into an office building for the government. The ghost that periodically appeared here was attached to the royal family in some way; it was seen by most of the descendants of the palace builder, the Margrave Frederick.

The appearance of the White Lady, as the ghost is known, goes back to 1619; she visited most of the

Margraves, electors and kings who ruled here, very much in the manner of an Irish banshee, warning of impending disaster or even speaking to the ruler about some event he needed to avoid. Usually, though, her appearance at infrequent intervals meant impending death to the ruler who encountered her. The last recorded appearance was in the bombed-out corridors of the Old Palace on April 29, 1945.

The former East German government destroyed the Old Palace's interior, but it has since been restored to all its former glory. That should please the White Lady, and perhaps she will walk again sometime.

How to get there
Now that Berlin's old center is being rebuilt, the Old Palace also is in the process of restoration, but easily accessible to visitors, smack in the middle of the former "official" Berlin, on the famous Unter den Linden Street.

Nearby accommodations
ECONTEL
Sömmeringstrasse. 24
Tel: 030/346-810 $

GENDARM GARNI HOTEL
Charlottenstrasse. 60
Tel: 030/204-4180 $

HOTEL CASINO
Königen-Elisabeth-Strasse 47a
Tel: 030/303-090 $$

Wolfsegg

Bayern, Germany

Because of the proximity of the River Danube, the fortress at Wolfsegg was always of importance. It rises majestically out of the valley to the equivalent of four or five modern stories. Constructed for defense, its thick bulky walls are forbidding, the small windows—high up to discourage aggressors—and the hill upon which the fortress perches making attack very difficult.

Wolfsegg never fell to an enemy, and even the formidable Swedes, who besieged it for a long time during the Thirty Years' War, gave up. Built in 1028, Wolfsegg belonged to several noble Bavarian families and was always directly or indirectly involved in intricate dynastic struggles among various lines of the Wittelsbach, who ruled Bayern, then called Bavaria, until 1918. Many of the masters of Wolfsegg made a living by being "Raubritter"—robber barons.

The late Georg Rauchenberger, painter and official guardian of monuments for the province of The Upper Palatinate (part of the state of Bavaria), purchased this ancient fortress with his own savings. On one occasion, Mr. Rauchenberger saw a young lady coming in with a small group of visitors, and when he turned to speak to her she disappeared. Therese Pielmeier, wife of the custodian, actually saw a whitish form in the yard, full of luminescence, and heard various unexplained noises.

Apparently, greedy relatives of a 14th-century owner of Wolfsegg had decided to take over the property, even then of considerable value, by trapping the young wife of the owner with another man. The husband, told of the rendezvous, arriving in time to see the two lovers together, killed both of them. The ghost that appears at Wolfsegg is the ghost of the murdered bride, perhaps trying to find her husband and appease his anger.

How to get there

Wolfsegg is now administered by the State of Bayern and is reached on secondary country roads in about an hour by car from the city of Regensburg, in central Bayern.

Nearby accommodations

ARCH
Haidplatz 4, Regensburg
Tel: (941) 502060 $$

BISCHOFSHOF AM DOM
Krauterermarkt 3, Regensburg
Tel: (941) 59086 $

GASTHOF STADLERBRAEU
Gewerbepark D90, Regensburg
Tel: (941) 40280 $$$

The Mysterious Death of King Ludwig II

Starnberg Lake, Munich, Germany

Bavaria's controversial King Ludwig II met an untimely death in Lake Starnberg, just southwest of his capital, Munich.

It was the mid-19th century, and the king's extravagant lifestyle was about to ruin his country: His sponsorship of Richard Wagner's expensive operas and the construction of several lavish fantasy castles were cause for serious alarm in the Royal Family. Eventually, his behavior became too much: he was deemed incapable of performing the functions of government and declared mentally unstable, placed under the care of a team of doctors and removed from Munich.

But he kept causing problems, demanding to return to his lifestyle and friends. One day, it was announced that the young king had accidentally drowned in Lake Starnberg. The only problem with this explanation was that the spot where he allegedly drowned while swimming is but a couple of yards from shore, where the water is only a few feet deep. Nobody can swim—or, for that matter, drown—there, unless someone held his head underwater long enough to accomplish that end.

A memorial church was built opposite the spot on shore, and a simple cross in the lake marks the exact spot of Ludwig's demise. But rumors about his death persist, and some travelers have reported running into a disheveled, silent, wet young man who strongly resembled the late King Ludwig.

How to get there

Today, the subway/elevated train system of Munich runs all the way out to the Starnberg Lake, about a half hour by train. The lake is just outside the city, to the southwest.

Nearby accommodations

ARABELLA CENTRAL
Schwanthalerstrasse 111, Munich
Tel: (89) 510830 $$

BEST WESTERN HOTEL CRISTAL
Schwanthalerstrasse 36, Munich
Tel: (89) 551110 $$

CARMEN
Hansastrasse 146, Munich
Tel: (89) 7601099 $$

The Shelbourne Hotel

Dublin, Ireland

My favorite hotel in Dublin, the Shelbourne, was built in 1824 by combining four brick homes facing St. Stephen's Green, in the most elegant section of the city. It is a grand old place, whose guest register has included everyone from the Dalai Lama to Princess Grace of Monaco to Laurel & Hardy.

In the lobby, visitors will find a blazing fire, huge brocade sofas and the classic energy of a bustling, luxurious hotel. No two guest rooms are the same, and all are furnished with fabulous antiques and lovely decor. The buildings have been expanded and refurbished twice in the last 20 years, and the results are stunning. Sit and have a drink in the Horse Shoe Bar or have a wonderful (but expensive) meal at the distinguished Aisling Restaurant.

In the old days, the top floor was where the servants lived. Today it is the penthouse suite and is considered a privileged location; I stayed there with my wife at the time and medium Sybil Leek. Sybil had an extraordinary encounter in her room, #526, with the ghost of a little girl who seemed about seven years old and said that her name was Mary Masters. She wanted to sleep with Sybil, but she kept saying that she was "looking for Sophie". Sybil had the impression this event had happened in 1846. This was definitely not a psychic imprint from the past, as so many ghostly experiences are—but a real, earthbound ghost, who needed to be released. Sybil tried to do just that, through seance and communication with the little girl.

If you stay in that room, perhaps the little girl will talk to you, but she may have found Sophie by now.

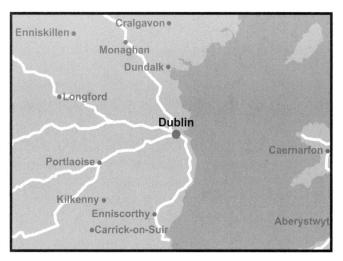

How to get there

The Shelbourne Hotel is of course a major Dublin landmark, and if you can, try to get room #526, or in any event, a room on the top floor.

Nearby accommodations

SHELBOURNE HOTEL
27 St. Stephen's Green
Tel: 01/676-6471 or (800) 225-5843 $$$

CENTRAL HOTEL
1-5 Exchequer Street
Tel: 01/679-7302 $

KILLINEY CASTLE
Killiney, Co. Dublin, (13 km from Dublin)
Tel: 01/284-0700 $$

The Ghost
of the Olympia Theatre

Dublin, Ireland

"I've heard some very curious tappings and bangings," Lorna Moran began, "and doors being shaken when they were very heavily chained. I have heard windows rattle outside the room where I was sitting, and when I came out I realized there was no window!"

Alfo O'Reilly, theater designer, said, "On the evening in question, Lorna and I worked very late into the night, and I had not heard any stories at all about this theatre being haunted. We went to up to the dressing room and we were sitting there quietly exhausted when we heard these incredible noises. We knew there was only one person in the theater, the night watchman, who was roaming elsewhere, and we were alone upstairs. There was certainly nothing in the corridor that could create this kind of noise."

Said Jeremy Swan, "I used to work here as resident stage manager. One season, during a pantomime, the dressing room was wrecked, allegedly by a poltergeist. All the clothes were strewn about, makeup was thrown all around the place. We questioned all the chorus girls who were in the room at the time—that was number 9 dressing room.

Apparently, there had been knocking at the door every night and nobody there, at half past nine. One night when I was working here as assistant to Miss Moran I went upstairs to the washroom, and when I came out, I saw a light—just a yellow glow; it seemed to be in the corner of the corridor. I followed the light around the corner, and it went into the corridor where number 9 was, where there was another door. The door was open, and it closed in my face!

"As a matter of fact, there was a civilian shot in the area—he was suspected of I.R.A. activities, but it was discovered afterwards that he had something to do with the Quartermaster stores down in Ironbridge Barracks. He was shot by mistake."

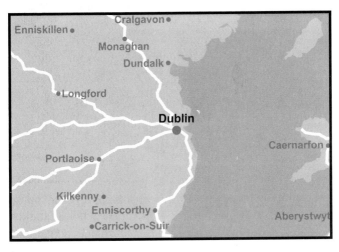

How to get there

The Olympia is in the heart of Dublin; at 72 Dame Street. You can call them for more information at 677-7744 for tickets, or 478-2183 for the Marketing & PR Office.

Nearby accommodations

SHELBOURNE HOTEL
27 St. Stephen's Green
Tel: 01/676-6471 or (800) 225-5843 $$$

CENTRAL HOTEL
1-5 Exchequer Street
Tel: 01/679-7302 $

KILLINEY CASTLE
Killiney, Co. Dublin, (13 km from Dublin)
Tel: 01/284-0700 $$

West Town House

Naul, County Dublin, Ireland

West Town House is an abandoned Greathouse not far from Dublin. It must have been a magnificent manor house at one time, but like so many, was left to die of neglect.

A Dublin couple who wandered into its ruins not long ago experienced a presence close enough to feel on their necks. Sybil Leek practically ran away when we set foot upon the shattered floor of the house. In a semi-trance she relived a scene from Ireland's past: A group of people had met here, she explained, who were considered rebels in their day because they advocated the establishment of a parliamentary government, or dail, in Ireland at a time when Ireland had not yet obtained her freedom from England. Apparently a young man by the name of Trehayne was among them. They found him to be a traitor and sentenced him to die.

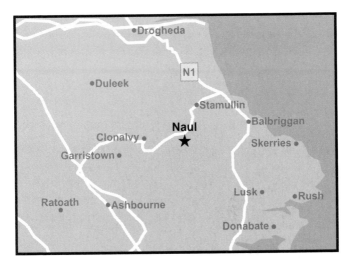

How to get there

The way to West Town House is not simple; it's easy to miss the entrance into the wilderness surrounding the manor. Going north on N1—the main Dublin-Belfast road (closest to the coast)—exit just before the town of Naul. Naul is right on the border between County Meath and County Dublin, about 10 km from the coast. The estate itself is about two kilometers off the road, beyond a gamekeeper's lodge, and is completely neglected. Eventually you will find yourself in front of the Greathouse.

Nearby accommodations

SHELBOURNE HOTEL
27 St. Stephen's Green
Tel: 01/676-6471 or (800) 225-5843 $$$

CENTRAL HOTEL
1-5 Exchequer Street
Tel: 01/679-7302 $

KILLINEY CASTLE
Killiney, Co. Dublin, (13 km from Dublin)
Tel: 01/284-0700 $$

Maynooth Seminary
County Kildare, Ireland

About an hour southwest of Dublin is the Roman Catholic seminary and college, Maynooth. In addition to its architectural attractions, Maynooth offers a ghost story, and while the church is not exactly thrilled about it, neither do they deny it.

In fact, students at the College make fun of the tradition at times. Rhetoric House, an important campus building, is where the events took place that led to the haunting of room #2. Sometime in the 1840s, a student living there committed suicide by cutting his wrists. Subsequently another student assigned to this room also committed suicide. The third student to live in the haunted room woke up from a vivid dream one morning with a razor in hand about to slit his own wrists. Realizing that his room and the spirits there had taken him over, he panicked and jumped out the window, but survived. No student would sleep in the room after that, but a priest volunteered to do so. The following morning, his hair had turned white and he was incoherent with fear.

College authorities then closed the room to students and turned it into an oratory to St. Joseph.

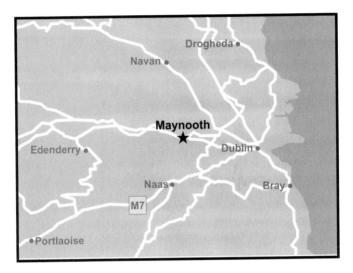

How to get there

Maynooth is best visited by car; it is about an hour's drive on the T3 road from Dublin. Visitors are admitted during daytime hours. Look for room #2 on the top floor of the Oratory of St. Joseph in Rhetoric House.

Nearby accommodations

MOYGLARE MANOR
Maynooth
Tel: (1) 6286351 $$$

KILLINEY CASTLE
Killiney, Co. Dublin, (13 km from Dublin)
Tel: 01/284-0700 $$

Kilkea Castle
County Kildare, Ireland

Kilkea, built in 1180 by an Anglo-Norman knight named Sir Walter de Riddleford, is the oldest inhabited castle in. Let there be no mistake: The inside has been modified and very little of the original castle remains. But the haunting is still there.

The haunted area is what must have been a servant's quarters, reached through a narrow passage in the northern section of the castle. The room itself is just large enough for one person; if you should want to sleep in it, you must make a reservation far in advance.

The story of the haunting goes back to the early Middle Ages. Apparently one of the beautiful daughters of an early owner fell in love with a stableboy. Her proud father disapproved and threatened to kill them both if they continued their association. One night, he found the young man in his daughter's room. In the struggle that followed the boy was killed; we are not told if the girl was also. The boy's ghost apparently still roams the corridors, trying to get back his sweetheart.

A number of people have reported uncanny feelings here. The owner of Kilkea himself, though skeptical, has admitted to witnessing doors opening by themselves for no apparent reason.

The facilities include an excellent dining room, d'Lacy's Restaurant, a bar, banquet and conference facilities, an indoor heated swimming pool, sauna, jacuzzi, steamroom and fully equipped gym. An 18 hole golf course encircles the Castle, and there are excellent tennis courts, trout streams and Equestrian facilities nearby.

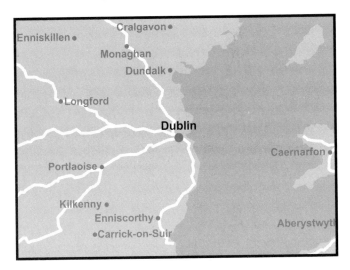

How to get there

Kilkea Castle is just southeast of Dublin, in the beautiful County Kildare. It can be easily and quickly reached by car, and the drive down the coast is quite-memorable.

Nearby accommodations

KILKEA CASTLE
Castledermot, County Kildare
Tel: 0503-45156 Fax: 0503-45187 $$$

The I.R.A. Ghosts

Listowel, County Kerry

On the road beyond Listowel, there is a monument to a tragedy in Ireland's struggle for independence. It is a large Celtic cross, set back from the road, and behind it are the graves of three I.R.A. men who died here in an ambush by British soldiers in 1918.

Just a few weeks after the men were buried, a 17-year-old lad named Patrick Maloney and his friend Moss Barney, were returning late one night from a dance. They were in a hurry to get home, since the area was not a particularly safe place to be at night. Several months had passed since the death of three I.R.A. sentries at that lookout, and the struggle was still in full swing.

When they reached the spot where the men are buried, they were stopped in their tracks. Their bicycles would not move an inch farther, as if an unseen force were holding onto them. At the same time, they felt a strong warning not to go farther down the road. Then the force released them, having delivered its message. Clearly, the dead men were still manning the lookout!

Today there is a striking stone monument at the exact spot where the I.R.A. soldiers are buried and where Barney & Maloney were halted. It is an impressive Celtic cross and a powerful reminder of the struggles between Ireland and England.

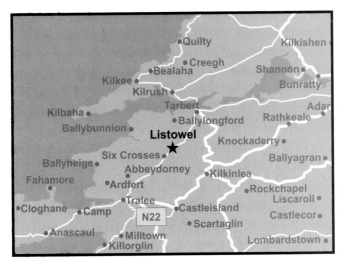

How to get there

The monument is right off the main road just after you leave (heading south) the town of Listowel, which is in County Kerry, south of Limerick.

Nearby accommodations

GREENHILLS
Ennis Road, Limerick
Tel: (61) 453033 $$

THE LIMERICK RYAN CONFERENCE CENTER
Ennis Road, Limerick
Tel: (61) 453922 $$

WOODFIELD HOUSE
Ennis Road, Limerick
Tel: (61) 53022 $

The Danish Sailor at Ballyheigue

County Kerry, Ireland

Ballyheigue was already old in 1730, when the Kerry records of that time show that a Danish ship called The Golden Lyon was passing by this part of the coast on her way back from the Indies to Denmark. She was blown off-course by a storm and could be plainly seen from the land. The Crosbies, owners of Ballyheigue Castle at that time, set up false lights on horses' heads to lure the ship even closer to shore, and sure enough, she was wrecked on the rocky Kerry coast. Thereupon Sir Thomas Crosbie sent out a crew to rescue the sailors of the Danish ship and salvage what was left of her cargo, which included 12 cases of silver bars and coin. The cargo was safely stored in the vaults of Ballyheigue Castle, and the survivors treated as honored guests, although they were, in essence, prisoners.

A year later, Sir Thomas had died, but the captain was still at Ballyheigue Castle—and so was the silver.

One night he was awakened by the sound of voices, and saw 50 or 60 men with blackened faces storming the castle gates. Lady Margaret, Sir Thomas' widow, begged the captain not to oppose the raiders or he might be killed. The raiders took away the silver chests and left many of the Danes dead. Most were later caught and some executed, but the silver was never completely recovered; no one knows where three-quarters of it went. Some say it was buried nearby.

In 1962, a Captain P. D. O'Donnell arrived at Ballyheigue on vacation. On the anniversary of the raid, he took snapshots in the ruined castle. Imagine his surprise when one of the pictures showed—in addition to the captain's very-much-alive nephew Frank—the figure of a Danish swordsman standing near a window! The figure wore high boots and clothes of the 18th century.

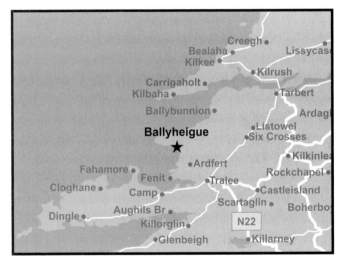

How to get there
Ballyheigue, in County Kerry (southwestern Ireland) lies right on the coast and is accessible almost exclusively by car. Take the L104 or the N20 from Limerick, then connect with the L105 to the village and then the ruins.

Nearby accommodations
WHITE SANDS
Ballyheigue. Tel: (66) 33102 $$

THE LIMERICK RYAN CONFERENCE CENTER
Ennis Road, Limerick. Tel: (61) 453922 $$

WOODFIELD HOUSE
Ennis Road, Limerick. Tel: (61) 53022 $

Skryne Castle
County Meath, Ireland

Skryne is an imposing building, especially when one drives up from the village and sees it looming behind the ancient trees on each side of the driveway. Apparently the present owners use the house for catering now and again, renting it out for wedding parties and such. It is therefore only semi-private—one can make arrangements for a visit.

The upstairs salon to the right of the staircase was the area Sybil Leek felt to be the most haunted. There were several layers of ghostly happenings in the atmosphere, she explained, one having to do with a courier arriving at the house half-dead from exhaustion and exposure and unable to be saved. That ghost goes back to the Middle Ages. Sybil had the impression that the man spoke of the fianna, a group of nobles who had rebelled against the high king Cairbre around A.D. 597, and that a battle had been fought between the rebels and the king at the very foot of Skryne Castle.

The specter inside the house, however, was female. The girl's name was Lilith Palmerston, and the tragedy that ended her life happened in 1740 when the Skryne was owned by Sir Bromley Casway. Lilith was his beautiful ward; during her long stay at Skryne she met a young man named Phelim Sellers, who lived not far from the castle. Unfortunately he fell in love with Lilith, who did not return his feelings. Finally Sir Bromley decided to take her to Dublin to escape the attentions of the unwanted suitor. The night before their planned departure, however, Sellers got wind of their intent, broke into Skryne Castle, entered the girl's room and strangled her. He was hanged for his crime at Galway City.

It is the girl's unhappy presence that has been felt on many occasions by those who have slept in her room. One man saw what he thought was a nun, who dissolved before his eyes. A woman who often worked in the castle heard footsteps when no one was walking.

How to get there

Driving up the T35 from Dublin north toward Belfast, you will come to the T26, which will take you along the River Boyne to the village of Skyrne, just past Drogheda.

Nearby accommodations

BOYNE VALLEY
Stameen, Drogheda
Tel: (41) 37737 $

The Haunted Rectory
Carlingford, County Louth, Ireland

The first time I heard of the haunted rectory at Carlingford was in August 1965, when its then-owner, the artist Ernest McDowell, approached me on the advice of an American friend who knew my work.

"The house was built in the seventeenth century," he began. "It was then a private house, a mansion that belonged to the Stannus family, before it was bought by the Church of Ireland for a rectory.

"One summer afternoon—early September, I recall—my brother and I were at the rectory. My brother was out cutting corn, and I was mowing the lawn. It was rather a hot evening and I thought I was getting a cold. I was very busy, though, and I just happened to look up towards the door, when I noticed moving toward it a figure of a girl in a red dress. I looked towards the gate that lets you into the grounds from the road—and coming in the gate was a clergy-man with a very high collar, and he vanished, too!

"Canon Meissner, who lived in the house for some time, saw the same girl in one of the rooms. She appeared to him on a separate occasion."

I have heard footsteps in the corridors, mainly upstairs, when I was quite alone in the house.

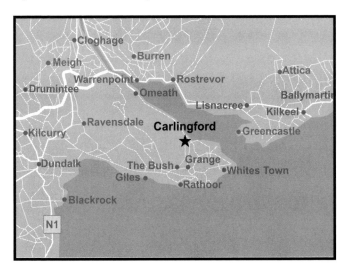

How to get there

Inquire about the rectory once you reach Carling-ford. The town lies on the coast just north of Dundalk Bay. Take the T1 to Dundalk, then the T62 directly into Carlingford village.

Nearby accommodations

McKevitt's Village
Market Square, Carlingford
Tel: (42) 73116 $

Imperial
Park Street, Dundalk
Tel: (42) 32241 Fax: (42) 37909 $

Carlingford Abbey
Carlingford, County Louth, Ireland

Carlingford Castle and Abbey—or what's left of them, which isn't much but ruins—stand near the shore of Lough Carlingford in northeastern Ireland, facing Britain across the sea in one direction and Northern Ireland in the other. The sea can be quite rough at times in this bay, and there is a romantic wildness to the scenery. Walking amidst the ruins of what was once an imposing castle and abbey, one gets the feeling of time standing still—and also sometimes of an eerie presence.

An English traveler, totally unaware of the haunting reported here, saw the shadowy figures of a woman and a man standing in what was once a chapel; he said that they merged, then disappeared into the night.

The explanation may be that in the first part of the 15th century, a female pirate named Henrietta Travescant, after giving up the sea, retired to Carlingford Abbey to serve as its head. Her ship in her active pirate days had been called The Black Abbess, so she took the same name when she became abbess of Carlingford. Perhaps what prompted her to give up the sea was not only her patriotic desire to give her ship to King Henry V, to serve in his war against France, but also her unhappiness at the loss of her beloved Nevin O'Neill, whom the cruel sea had taken during one of their expeditions. It is her ghost and O'Neill's who have been seen walking by the rocky seashore or standing together in the ruined chapel.

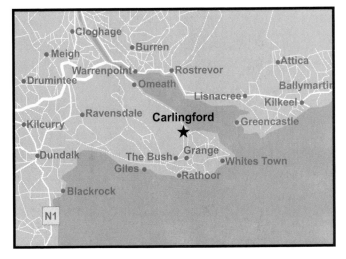

How to get there

The ruins can be reached on foot only, from the village near the shore of Lough (Lake) Carlingford. The town lies on the coast just north of Dundalk Bay. Take the T1 to Dundalk, then the T62 directly into Carlingford village.

Nearby accommodations

McKevitt's Village
Market Square, Carlingford
Tel: (42) 73116 $

Imperial
Park Street, Dundalk
Tel: (42) 32241   Fax: (42) 37909 $

Renvyle House
County Galway, Ireland

Renvyle House is a first-rate hotel looking out onto the westernmost tip of Ireland. The accommodations are first-class, though limited, because Renvyle House is not very large.

Originally, the estate was the seat of the Blake family. But they moved over 200 years ago, and a great deal of the most interesting (and well-documented) history and haunting here are associated with the family of Oliver St. John Gogarty, the famous literary figure. The first Gogarty House burned down during the so-called "Troubles." Although the present structure was built in 1932, it seems to have inherited some of the haunting of the past.

The haunted rooms seem to be Numbers 27, 2, and possibly 38. The first manifestation was after a seance held during St. John Gogarty's ownership, when one of the Blake children evidently materialized before the astonished assembly.

Additionally, in 1966, a maid saw a man in one of the upstairs corridors disappear into thin air before her eyes. When she described the stranger, it became clear that she was describing the late poet W. B. Yeats, who considered Renvyle House a second home.

Also of interest nearby are the ruins of the ancient Renvyle Castle—once the home of the 16th century pirate queen, Grania O'Malley.

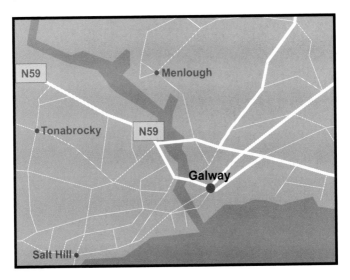

How to get there

Renvyle is just outside of on the westernmost tip of Ireland, on Clew Bay. Take the T71 to Letterfrack, then follow the signs to Renvyle.

Nearby accommodations

RENVYLE HOUSE
Tel: (95) 43511 Fax: (95) 43515 $$

GLENLO ABBEY HOTEL
Bushypark, Galway.
Tel: (91) 526666 $$$

The Ghosts of Fortezza

Hotel Post Reifer, South Tyrol, Italy

Fortezza (or in German, Franzensfeste), an ancient Austrian Imperial fortress town, is in the South Tyrol, a province of Italy formerly part of the Austrian empire and still mainly German-speaking.

The Hotel Post Reifer, built in the traditional Tyrolean style, has been a family-owned business since 1872. Today, it is one of the finest hotels in that part of Europe, easily accessible through the Brenner Pass, not far from the city of Brixen.

Two Americans, a couple named Leon and Mary, visited there on vacation; since Leon's father was from that area, they wanted to experience it. But the pLeesant, well-kept room they were given was anything but peaceful. During the night, voices kept waking them up, crying and expressing a need to escape something. The next morning, Leon and Mary left abruptly. Upon later investigation, the couple discovered that during World War II and the German occupation of Italy, the hotel was apparently under the control of the Gestapo. The room—and perhaps others—had been used to house prisoners on their way to concentration camps.

How to get there

Fortezza lies near the town of Sciaves in the Italian South Tyrol, and can be reached by car from either Meran or Bolzano on the A22.

Nearby accommodations

HOTEL POST REIFER
Trient-Sterling, Fortezza.
Tel: (047) 458605 $

GRIFONE GREIF
Waltherplatz 7, Bolzano.
Tel: (471) 977056
Fax: (471) 980613 $

REGINA ANGELORUM
Rittnerstrasse 1, Bolzano.
Tel: (471) 972195
Fax: (471) 972351 $$

Ghosts in the Dutch Capital

The Hague, The Netherlands

Den Haag, known in English as The Hague, is not only the official capital of The Netherlands and seat of their royal family, but also an ancient center of culture and diplomacy. Amsterdam may be the commercial center of this area, but The Hague is where history was made.

The building at #12, Westeinde, currently occupied by an auction house called Glerum CS, was formerly the seat of several foreign embassies, notably the British Embassy. In fact, one Ambassador, Sir Richard Adam Sykes, was ambushed and murdered in front of the building in 1979. Jan de Wit, during the struggle for Dutch independence, was a prisoner here in 1653.

The building is haunted by the ghost of Catherine de Chasseur, an 18th century French Huguenot noblewoman who resided there at one time. Several witnesses, including the British Ambassador Sir Horace Rumbold, have seen the apparition.

Also in The Hague, not too far away, is another

haunted house worthy of a visit. The Gevangenpoort Museum at Buitenhof 33, housed in another very old building, not only contains many interesting relics and artworks from Holland's great past, but also several ghosts. These do not seem to be connected with the exhibits here, but may be imprints from past events before the building was turned into a museum.

The Dutch attitude toward ghosts is rather practical: They are neither afraid of them nor do they make much of a fuss if and when they have such experiences. Both places can be freely visited, and questions about the ghosts are welcomed.

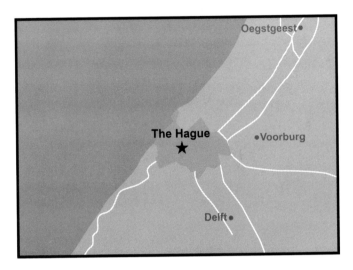

How to get there

Right in the center of The Hague, these two historical buildings can be visited during business hours without any problem. #12 Westeinde is now a busy auction house, and the Gevangenpoort Museum is also open to visitors during normal hours.

Nearby accommodations

HOLIDAY INN CROWN PLAZE DEN HAAG
Van Stolkweg 1
Tel: 31 (70) 3525161 $$

ATLANTIC
Deltaplein 200.
Tel: 31 (70) 32540035 $$

MERCURE CENTRAL
Spui 180.
Tel: 31 (70) 3636700 $$

Woodhouse Lee Ruins

Near Edinburgh, Scotland

Woodhouse Lee is just outside of Edinburgh, Scotland. There are, in fact, three sites in this area with the same name: the original site, which is now just a meadow with a few foundation stones where the original manor house stood; the original manor house that was moved from its original foundation to another hill nearby; and a new, private cottage that was named after the old manor house. Be sure, when you visit, not to confuse the ancient ruin and the nearby manor house with the cottage of the same name—the cottage is lovely, but it is the ruin and the manor house that are haunted.

I was drawn to visit there by rumors of a local legend about a "White Lady of Woodhouse Lee". With a little historical investigation and a visit, I learned that the haunting in this dense forest is very real. Now, the site of the old mansion is just a meadow with a few foundation stones scattered about.

Her name was Lady Anne Bothwell, and originally she lived at the old Woodhouse Lee Castle, which is about four miles from here. Once, when her husband was away, one of his enemies took over the castle and pushed her out, and she died in the snow. She appears in with nothing on because when she was forced out of her home, she was naked. Apparently her ghost made such a nuisance of itself that the owners decided to move the castle and brought most of the stones and built the mansion house called Woodhouse Lee up on the hill. Lady Anne's ghost appears in the meadow still, but her presence can be felt most strongly at the manor house.

She always appears at the same door on the north side of the building. The ghost is especially active on snowy nights—there have been fairly vigorous knocks on the door; and when someone goes outside to investigate, there is never anyone there—nor are there any footprints in the deep snow.

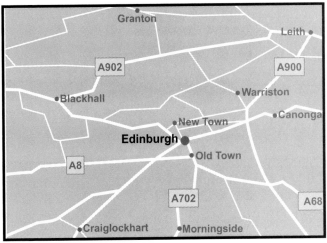

How to get there
The original ruins are on a hill just south of Edinburgh on the right side of A702 road.

Nearby accommodations
ELLESMERE GUEST HOUSE
11 Glengyle Terrace, Edinburgh
Tel: 0131/229-4823 $

LODGE HOTEL
6 Hampton Terrace, West Coates, Edinburgh
Tel: 0131/337-3682 $$

HOLIDAY INN CROWNE PLAZA
80 High Street, Royal Mile, Edinburgh
Tel: 0131/557-9797 or (800) 227-6963 $$$

Traquair House
Innerleithen, Scotland

Known as the "oldest inhabited house in Scotland," Traquair House at Innerleithen rises to five stories amid a majestic park. The magnificent castle dates back to the 12th century, and has been a retreat for 27 Scottish monarchs. There is a tradition that the magnificent gates of Traquair, topped with stone statues of fabled animals, shall remain closed until a Stuart king is crowned again in London (there are other ways of gaining entry to the house).

This Jacobite sentiment goes back to when the earls of Traquair supported the Stuart cause—the present lord, Peter Maxwell Stuart, is more concerned with the quality of the beer he brews. He's also the author of a magnificently illustrated booklet detailing the treasures at Traquair House. These include, in the traditional king's room, the bed in which Mary Queen of Scots slept, with a coverlet made by her ladies-in-waiting.

The former caretaker, Andrew Aiken Burns, who had been at the house since 1934, saw a lady in a Victorian dress walking on the grass. She walked slowly down through the gate and past a small cottage; then through the wicket gate into the garden—

but the gate was shut. This was Lady Louisa Stuart, who died in 1875 at 100. She is buried in a vault in the Traquair churchyard, right in back of the castle.

Besides the ghosts that appear here (the management encourages questions about the ghosts, and you can find more information about them at the gift shop), there is a maze, a famous 18th century brewery (still functioning), a variety of restaurant options, craft workshops, wooded walks and some wonderful antique shops. Inside, you'll find an amazing library, a vast collection of embroidered tapestries and a secret staircase used by Catholic priests hiding from Protestant persecution.

Traquair House is open daily between Easter Saturday and the end of September ; during October: Friday through Sunday only between the hours of 12:30pm-5:30pm; during June, July and August, the grounds are open from 10:30am-5:30pm daily. Call the Local Tourist Information Centre for more information: +44 (0)1721 720 138.

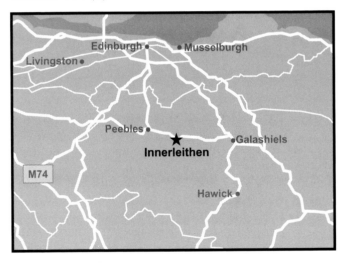

How to get there

Traquair lies 30 miles south of Edinburgh, 6 miles from Peebles and 1.5 miles from Innerleithen on B7062. The nearest railway station and airport are both in Edinburgh.

Nearby accommodations

CASTLE VENLAW HOTEL
Edinburgh Road, Peebles
Tel: 01721 720384
Fax: 01721 724066

The Castle Venlaw Hotel

Peebles, Scotland

Twenty-three miles from Edinburgh, in a fertile valley that was once the center of the mill industry but is now largely agricultural, stands the town of Peebles. In the surrounding countryside, Peebleshire, are many lovely vacation spots, quiet conservative villas and small hotels much favored by the English and Scots.

One such place is the Castle Venlaw Hotel, on a bluff 700 feet above sea level on the outskirts of town. Open for summer guests only, it gives the appearance of a castle. Standing four stories high, with a round tower in one corner, Venlaw was a fortified house rather than a heavy medieval fortress. Access is from the rear; behind the hotel. The present building was erected in 1782 on the site of an old Scottish keep called Smithfield Castle.

In the summer of 1968 an American couple decided to spend a few days at Venlaw Castle. "The room we occupied was at the end of the middle floor with a little turret room which my daughter used," Mrs. S. explained. "The very first night we were there, the room was ice-cold even though it was July, and we couldn't wait to close the lights and go to sleep. Immediately upon getting into bed, I suddenly heard a long, drawn-out and quite human sigh! It seemed to be near the foot of my bed."

"There are things we don't like to speak about," the hotel manager said. "We've had only one traumatic accident. About twenty years ago one of our guests fell from a bedroom window."

With its magnificent turrets and secluded grounds, the Castle Venlaw is a wonderful get-away spot that offers excellent service, food and accommodations in an old-fashioned family-run manner.

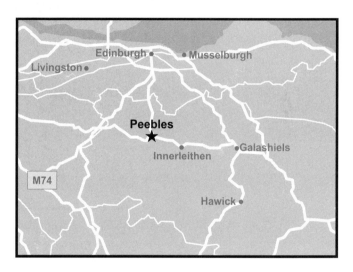

How to get there

The Castle Venlaw Hotel is a reasonably modern hotel popular with tourists, and there is an ancient ruin underneath it. Peebles is 23 miles south of Edinburgh; but travel by car is best. The hotel is off A703 Peebles/Edinburgh road, 0.75m from Peebles.

Nearby accommodations

Castle Venlaw Hotel
Edinburgh Road, Peebles
Tel: 01721 720384
Fax: 01721 724066

Hermitage Castle

Hawick, Scotland

The area on either side of the dividing line between Scotland and England is known as The Borders. It is somewhat wild and remote, and the roads are a little bit difficult to navigate. At night you can very easily get lost there, but it is well worth the drive down from Edinburgh to Hermitage Castle, located outside the town of Hawick.

The current castle, erected by master stonemason John Lewin of Durham, dates back to the 14th century, although there is evidence that another castle stood in the same spot a few hundred years earlier.

Centuries ago, nobody trusted the neighbors. Petty wars and family feuds were the rule among the nobles of Scotland. This area was no exception—throughout the 15th century, the English and the Scots battled endlessly over the ownership of the

Hermitage. When a neighboring chief sent a group of goodwill ambassadors to Hermitage to propose cessation of their long feud, the lord of the manor promptly put them into a small room without food or water, where they died miserably. Their ghosts are said to be among many who still stalk the ruins.

The Hermitage Castle is still very much covered with impressions from its cruel past. Not only are the unhappy spirits of the victims felt in the atmosphere by anyone sensitive enough, but there is also another reason Hermitage is different from other castles: One of its former owners, the Baron de Soulis, was a black magician who committed a number of documented atrocities, was boiled alive in a cauldron by the wise wizard Thomas of Ercildoune.

Surrounded by untouched open moorland, the Castle is run by Historic Scotland and is open to the public at the following times:

April 1 to Sept 30: Weekdays, 9.30-6.30, Sundays, 2.00-6.30.

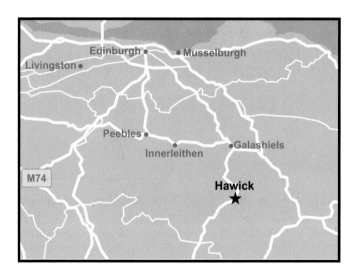

How to get there

Hermitage is in the Borders between Scotland and England, near the town of Hawick, about two hours south of Edinburgh by car, Hermitage can be freely visited.

Nearby accommodations

KIRKLANDS
West Stewart Place, Hawick
Tel: (1450) 372263 $$

Glamis Castle
Angus, Scotland

Glamis Castle's principal claim to fame is the fact that William Shakespeare placed his drama Macbeth there. The play is historically inaccurate, so Banquo's ghost may never appear at Glamis. But Glamis is haunted just the same.

This is the ancestral home of the Earls of Strathmore, and had also been the residence of the Scottish king, Malcolm II, who was allegedly murdered there in 1034. In 1372 the estate was given to Sir John Lyon by King Robert II, who titled him Thane of Glamis. (Thane is a title equivalent to Baron.) All of the royalty that used Glamis Castle until the 17th century used it primarily as a hunting lodge—between 1675 and 1687, the castle was extensively added to and remodeled.

The current royal family has a variety of connections to the place as well: HRH Queen Elizabeth spent her childhood there with HRH Princess Margaret (who was actually born in the castle) and the Queen Mother.

A traditional story tells of a room at Glamis no one is permitted to enter. A member of the Strathmore family was supposedly imprisoned there for life because of some deformity. His ghost has been seen and heard walking the corridors at night. No effort to contact the unhappy wraith has been made, especially as the administration of the castle frowns on any such attempt.

Now, the castle is open to the public; you'll find a restaurant, world-class collections of china and embroidery, a gift shop and extensive facilities for tourists. Guided tours are available.

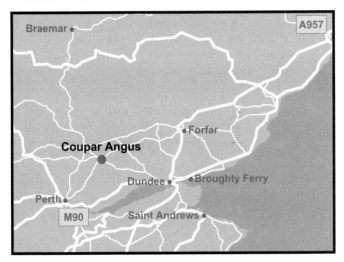

How to get there

Glamis is in Angus, on the A94 Highway, 6 miles west of Forfar, in the Highlands of Scotland. Open daily from March to October; and the area is best navigated by car.

Nearby accommodations

ROYAL ANGUS THISTLE
10 Marketgait, Dundee
Tel: 44 (1382) 26874 $$

THE QUEEN'S
160 Nethergate, Dundee
Tel: 44 (1382) 322515 $$

Culzean Castle

Ayr, Scotland

Culzean Castle rises sheer from the sea on the Ayrshire Coast in western Scotland. Its view is dramatic, looking out from its perch atop the cliffs South of Ayr to the spectacular bay, Arran and the Ailsa Craig.

Built by Robert Adam in 1792 for the 10th Earl of Cassillis, who wanted a place to entertain his friends, Culzean Castle has been restored extensively in keeping with Adam's style. Besides the Earl of Cassillis and his progeny, the castle has been associated with the Kennedy family and the Marquises of Ailsa, whose portraits are seen all over the castle.

Operated by the National Trust, the 560 acres of park and woodland at The Castle and grounds were presented to the Trust in 1945 by the Kennedy family. Today Culzean is operated by the National Trust—it is a museum and was declared a country park in 1969. the 560 acres of park & woodland, along with the Castle and its immediate grounds were presented to the National Trust by the Kennedy family in 1945.

Its main tower rises majestically four stories from the cliff, and one of the top floors contains an apartment dedicated to General Eisenhower as a gesture of gratitude from Britain. He stayed there with his family from time to time.

A British visitor to Culzean by the name of Margaret Penney was somewhat luckier—if seeing a ghost is luck. Mrs. Penney said the ghost was dark-haired and very beautiful. "She came down a corridor when I was visiting Culzean Castle recently, and said to me, 'It rains today.' She appeared to be in evening dress, though it was only about five o'clock in the afternoon when I encountered her. Anyway, I squeezed myself against the corridor to let her pass and told her, 'Not much room for passing when you're as plump as me.'"

Mrs. Penney said the girl looked at her very sadly and answered, "I do not require any room nowadays." Then, Mrs. Penney's entire right side went cold. "Suddenly I realized she had walked through my side!"

How to get there

Culzean (pronounced "Cullane") is on the western seashore off the A719, 4 miles west of Maybole and 12 miles south of Ayr (pronounced "air"). This is a major tourist attraction and there are guides. It is also possible to rent an "apartment" here during the season.

Nearby accommodations

THE CALEDONIAN
Dalblair Road, Ayr
Tel: (1292) 269331
Fax: (1292) 610722 $$

The
Haunted Former Hospital
Zurich, Switzerland

The house in question is now a private residence, but also serves as headquarters of the Swiss Society for Parapsychology. The society is headed by Zurich psychiatrist Dr. Hans Negele-Osjord and is headquartered at #127 Hoenger Strasse.

Rather aristocratic in design and appearance, the house stands on upper Hoenger Street at a spot where it overlooks much of downtown Zurich. It is a square, heavy-set stone house with three stories, and an attic above the top story. In this attic there is a window that does not want to stay closed—no matter how often one tries to close it.

On the third floor, there is a small room which for many years has served as a maid's room. It was here that the most notable phenomena have been observed. A maid named Liesl saw a man standing between the bed and the wall with a candle in his hand. She panicked and ran from the room screaming in terror. Another servant girl took Liesl's place. A year and a half after the initial incident, the new girl saw the same apparition.

The explanation is this: during the seventeenth century the house had been a military hospital. Many wounded soldiers who came there died. The cap worn by the apparition was the soldier's cap worn in the period. Most likely the man is lost between two states of being and would like to get out—if only someone would show him the way.

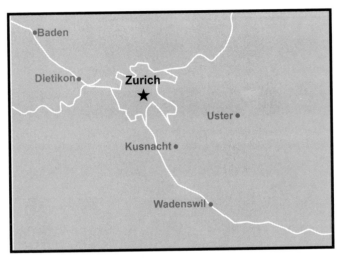

How to get there

The house at 127 Hoenger Strasse in Zurich is private, but no one will stop you from having a look from the outside.

Nearby accommodations

GLOCKENHOF
Sihlstrasse 31
Tel: 01/211-56-50
Fax: 01/211-56-60 $

SONNENBERG
Aurorastrasse 98
Tel: 01/262-00-62
Fax: 01/262-06-33 $$

CENTRAL PLAZA
Central 1
Tel: 01/251-55-55
Fax: 01/251-85-35 $$$

Haunted Basel Cathedral

Basel, Switzerland

For years, people who visited the majestic Gothic cathedral in Basel, in the middle of the city, have reported strange feelings when standing near one of the massive pillars which rise high to support the roof of the great church.

When I visited Basel Cathedral some years ago, I took black and white photographs that included the pillars in the area where people had reported "strange feelings." Picture my surprise when one shot clearly showed a human skeleton in a crouched position!

During the Middle Ages, clergy who had broken their vows were sometimes sealed alive in the wall of a church as punishment. The pillar with the skeleton in it is on the left side of the nave, as you look from the altar toward the rear of the church.

Whether the church is still haunted by a trapped spirit or whether the image was merely an impression from the past is difficult to say; only future witnesses can shed light on this.

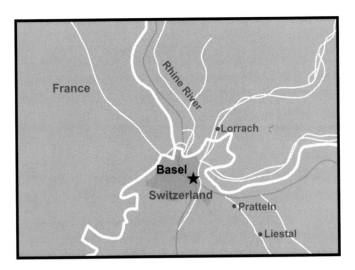

How to get there

Basel Cathedral, in the heart of the city, is nearly always open to visitors. You may get some psychic impressions by walking near the pillars that support the roof of the nave.

Nearby accommodations

ADMIRAL BASEL
Rosenthalstrasse 5/Am Messeplatz
Tel: (61) 6917777
Fax: (61) 6917789 $$

BASEL
Münzgasse 12
Tel: (61) 2646800
Fax: (61) 2646811 $$$

DRACHEN
Aeschenvorstadt 24
Tel: (61) 2729090
Fax: (61) 2729002 $$

Ghostly Sightings

Site:

Date:

Manifestation:

Notes:

Site:

Date:

Manifestation:

Notes:

Site:

Date:

Manifestation:

Notes:

Site:

Date:

Manifestation:

Notes:

Site:

Date:

Manifestation:

Notes:

Site:

Date:

Manifestation:

Notes:

Site:

Date:

Manifestation:

Notes:

Site:

Date:

Manifestation:

Notes:

Site:

Date:

Manifestation:

Notes:

Site:

Date:

Manifestation:

Notes: